New Nations and Peoples

Scandinavia

Scandinavia

W. R. MEAD & WENDY HALL

with 31 illustrations and a map

THAMES AND HUDSON · LONDON

© Thames and Hudson Ltd. 1972

Photoset in Great Britain by
Filmtype Services Limited, Scarborough, England

Printed and bound in Great Britain by Cox and Wyman Ltd,
London, Fakenham and Reading.

ISBN 0 500 12027 7

Contents

Part One   The Scandinavian background

1   The Nordic scene

THE FIVE COUNTRIES Denmark, Finland, Iceland, Norway and Sweden are together popularly known to the outside world as Scandinavia. Geography, history and language have linked them in incomplete or shifting systems which have created, through the centuries, different relationships and different tensions. Through geography Norway and Sweden share the Scandinavian peninsula, and Sweden and Finland share a common border. Only the narrow channel of the Sound separates Denmark from south Sweden; but Iceland lies away in the North Atlantic, six hundred miles from Norway.

Until this century history has divided the five countries into the dominant and the dominated. Denmark and Norway were united under one crown for several centuries, with Denmark as the dominant partner until its place was taken by Sweden. In 1905 Norway separated from Sweden and became once again a sovereign state. Finland was for more than six hundred years a part of the kingdom of Sweden, and then a Grand Duchy of Russia from 1809 to 1917, when it became independent. Iceland was linked with Denmark until 1944. Thus in the twentieth century Scandinavia has become a varied group of three monarchies – Denmark, Sweden and Norway – and two republics, Finland and Iceland. Between these five the new relationships of sovereign and equal states have had to be worked out, and the inherited tensions of history relaxed.

The ties of race and language are fundamentally strong. All, except a majority of Finns, are Nordics; all, except a majority of Finns, speak a related Norse language. Since the 1930s the five countries have come to call themselves collectively 'Norden' (the North), the name indicating the community that they have created. Although the word 'Norden', with its associated adjectival forms, is both explicit and felicitous in the languages and literatures of the five countries, it has not acquired a popular appeal in the world at large. When translated it lacks precision. In its original form, the word 'Norden' could be easily assimilated into English and other Germanic languages, but it has so far failed. It could not be assimilated in spelling or pronunciation into the Latin tongues, which all long ago adopted and adapted with ease their own versions of the word 'Scandinavia'.

Scandinavia has been called 'the quiet corner of Europe'. By comparison with most parts of the world, its member states live in harmony with each other and generally contrive to avoid disharmony with their non-Scandinavian neighbours. There are geographical facts which favour a unity of interests among the five countries and help to foster this harmony. Some of these facts have operated in a common manner throughout history; some have experienced re-interpretation with changes in technology. Some spring from narrower domestic circumstances; some are written in the relationship of the Scandinavian area to the broader European scene and world setting. By contrast, there are geographical facts which work against Scandinavian unity. These, too, are expressions of international setting as well as well as of domestic circumstance. These, too, change with technological change.

There are two basic facts of physical geography which create common problems and which favour co-operative endeavour in their solutions. They are a high-latitude location and a maritime setting. At large and in detail, the consequences of these characteristics are fundamental, though their precise qualities differ from country to country and, indeed, within individual countries. A third fact common to all five countries, but different in emphasis from country to country, is the uneven distribution of their resources.

The facts of latitude are impressive. About a third of the land area of Norway and more than a quarter of the surface areas of Sweden and Finland are north of the Arctic Circle. The capital cities Oslo, Stockholm and Helsinki lie approximately on the sixtieth line of latitude north: Reykjavik and Trondheim are on latitude 64°N. Viewed globally, the most densely peopled and fully developed parts of Norway, Sweden and Finland lie in the same latitudes as the Ungava peninsula of Labrador or the Russian peninsula of Kam-

8

chatka. Denmark, too, is familiar with high-latitude experience, for its Arctic dependency of Greenland is larger than Scandinavia in its entirety.

High latitude explains the pronounced seasonal rhythm of daylight and darkness that is such a distinguishing feature of Scandinavia. The mental picture of the area is inseparable from midnight sun and light nights, from midwinter darkness and *Aurora borealis*. In their acting, if not always in their thinking, the north is the primary compass point for the Scandinavians. It was natural that the literature of environmental determinism should concern itself with the antitheses of gloom and radiance, and that ice and snow should be influential components. The ice cathedral was the climax of Henrik Ibsen's *Brand* and *The Ice Palace* is the title of one of the tragedies of Tarjei Vesaas (1897–1970). Hans Christian Andersen's Snow Queen resided in Lapland and, since reindeer draw his sleigh, Father Christmas has more recently acquired an address beside her.

Winter darkness and cold (and the antitheses of midsummer light and warmth) are inescapable realities; yet the Scandinavian countries escape relatively lightly by comparison with the climatic severities experienced by most territories in their latitudes. In the same way as Alaska and British Columbia are located on the west coast of north America, the Scandinavian countries occupy the north-western coastlands of Eurasia. Accordingly, they are located in the main stream of the cyclonic systems that swing across the north Atlantic. Although these systems commonly create a negative human impression with their rain and cloud, their air masses, having passed over several thousands of miles of relatively warm water, are correspondingly warm. At the same time, the circulation of the north Atlantic itself is such that the warm surface drift of the ocean current popularly known as the Gulf Stream also helps to ameliorate the climate of most of Scandinavia. On climatic grounds, the great peninsula of Quebec-Labrador has been called a part of the sub-Arctic trespassing into temperate latitudes. By contrast, much of Scandinavia can be regarded as a part of the temperate zone intruding upon the Arctic and sub-Arctic. This is especially evident in Norway, where many coastal areas have the most favoured temperatures of any part of the world for their latitudes. The consequences are seen in the vegetation – marine as well as terrestrial. Beech trees and a flora reminiscent of the English downlands thrive around the shores of Trondheimfjord;

while the skerry channels off Bergen flaunt fragile corals and the waters off Arctic Norway are among the richest areas of marine life in the world.

Baltic Scandinavia as well as Atlantic Scandinavia shares the cyclonic experience, though here the physical influences of the Atlantic system are weakened when they encounter those of continental Eurasia. This makes for differences between eastern and western Scandinavia – from climate, through vegetation, to rural economic opportunity. These differences are exaggerated from south to north.

A direct consequence of the high temperature anomaly of Atlantic Scandinavia is high humidity. Rain, cloud, mist and fog are characteristic, especially of the highland coasts of Norway, Iceland and the Atlantic islands. When gales and squalls are added they become veritable Flying Dutchman country. For Atlantic Scandinavia can be windy as well as wet. The windiness of the plains of Jutland is proverbial: seed grain can be blown away after the sowing. The wind-trimmed trees to the east of the wandering duneland fringe of Denmark's virtually harbourless North Sea coast are living expressions of the westerly airstream. South-west Iceland and north Norway have some of the highest recorded wind speeds. Not surprisingly their skerries and seaward-facing mountain flanks are bare of trees. Wind and high humidity are the more disagreeable when combined with low temperatures. The black ice that settles upon trawlers and fishing boats in high latitudes is probably the ultimate climatic hazard, while ice storms are a complementary hazard for territory that relies heavily for its various communicational systems on overhead wires. Cloud is abundant, sunshine is restricted. Sunshine hours fall to a minimum of the possible in parts of western Iceland. In many places in western Norway the low sunshine potential is reduced yet further by the shadowing effects of mountain walls.

In eastern Scandinavia cloud gives way to more frequent sunshine. March is usually radiant and, with the continental high pressure at a maximum, stable sunny weather often extends westwards beyond the North Sea to eastern England. The summers of Baltic Scandinavia can often attain a Mediterranean intensity, giving to the limestone walls and towers of a city such as Visby the illusion of classical Ilium. Finland can be drawn into the orbit of the Russian summer, experiencing the hot south-eastern winds that drive up from the steppelands. A direct consequence of this accumulation of heat can be thunderstorms, which are the principal cause of summer fires in the forests of Finland and Sweden.

While the cloud cover of much of western Scandinavia prevents excessive radiation in winter, clear skies in eastern Scandinavia produce plummeting temperatures. As the aircraft flies, the central Baltic is less than a thousand miles from London, but in February or March it conveys the impression of polar latitudes. The brackish Baltic Sea supports an ice cover the extent of which reflects the intensity of winter cold. The inner reaches of the Gulfs of Bothnia and Finland are frozen in early December and are rarely free until mid-May. In very hard winters, which may occur on an average once a decade, a virtually continuous ice cover may push into the Kattegat, though in mild winters the ice cover may not extend beyond the Åland Sea. It can be midsummer before the ice floes disappear from the central Bothnian Gulf. While ice provides the drama in Baltic Scandinavia, snow is its complement in Norway. It is measured in metres. In the same way as icebreakers yield to conditions in the Gulf of Bothnia, snow ploughs frequently have to succumb to the volume of snow that accumulates on Norway's fells. Some of the main highways across the western plateaux are closed for several months. It goes without saying that, against the background of such experiences, the Scandinavians have a world status as experts on the problems of ice and snow.

The movement of air masses, the circulation of surrounding waters and the rhythm of the seasons may seem remote facts in the explanation of Scandinavian situations, but they are bold realities in the background to daily life. They are universals in time and place though their incidence differs regionally and locally. Their incidence also changes in time, and long-term climatic changes have been influential features in Scandinavian history. The Scandinavians have been and remain the more sensitive to these changes because so much of their territory lies in the frontier areas of human settlement.

This territory differs greatly in character from country to country. Denmark is geologically a young country whose soft chalk cliffs rise above the shallow Baltic Sea or emerge from the thick covering of glacial deposits that give to eastern Jutland in particular a hilly character. Denmark is also a low-lying country. Himmelbjerget, its high point, only attains a modest 550 feet. By contrast, Finland is a geologically old country where the consequences of the Ice Age are inscribed in erosion rather than in deposition. As with Denmark, it is low-lying and its granite bedrocks only exceed 1,000 feet in the northern quarter of the country. Iceland, whose dark basaltic rocks have been – and are being – born of fire, is a lofty island, though youthful in geological terms. Norway, loftiest of all, is geologically comparable in age and form with north-west Scotland. Sweden shares the geology of Norway, of Finland and, marginally in the extreme south-west, of Denmark.

The facts of geology control resources both directly and indirectly. Different types of rocks contain different mineral endowments. Iceland's bedrocks contain no minerals of consequence. Denmark has abundant chalk which is the basis for a major cement industry, but has little else save for the little-known mineralogical potential of Greenland. The old rocks of the Fennoscandian shield are the repository of a variety of minerals, though their volume differs pronouncedly from place to place. Sweden is rich in minerals, especially in iron ores, and Swedish Lapland is one of Europe's leading sources of phosphoric ores. Related iron mountains occur in adjacent Finnish and Norwegian Lapland, though the size of their deposits is much smaller and the quality generally lower. Finland, Sweden and Norway all have copper-bearing ores, with Finland's pyritic mine at Outokumpu claiming a leading role in European output. In both volume and variety of ores, Sweden takes precedence.

Yet all five countries suffer a major deficiency of combustible fuels. Sweden has a few small coal mines in the extreme south-west: it has also limited oil shales. Norway has coal mines in austere and isolated Spitsbergen. Denmark has inefficient brown coal. Nor are the generally abundant supplies of peat an efficient source of energy. Iceland has very substantial thermal energy in its unharnessed steam springs (or solfataras) for the development of which New Zealand experiences provide models. Both Denmark and Norway anticipate a quota of North Sea gas and oil.

But energy is available from falling water, so that geology helps to provide a different kind of energy in a different way. Hydro-electric power is a direct expression of topography and climate. The differences in slope, run-off and precipitation conditions from country to country result in pronounced differences in potential. Low-lying Denmark has very little hydro-electric energy. Norway and Sweden are among the leaders of European production. Iceland has a high

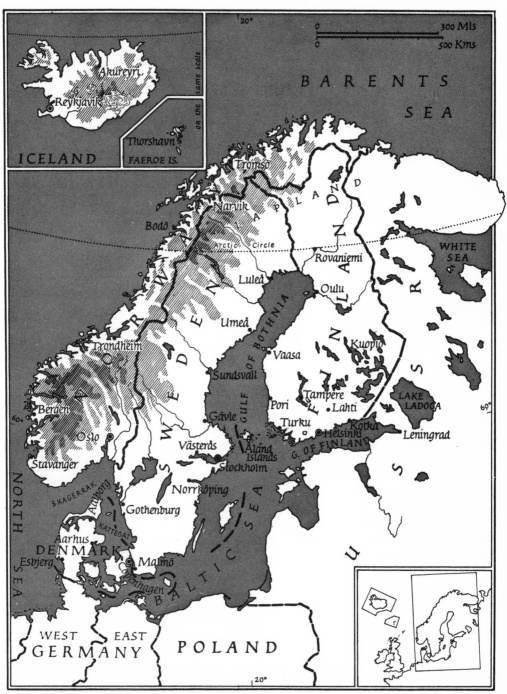

The Scandinavian countries: land over 1500 ft and 3000 ft shaded

undeveloped potential; Finland's modest resources are almost completely harnessed. All in all, geological differences account for some of the primary distinctions between the modern states of Scandinavia.

Rocks make a topographical impact through variations in relief: they make an economic impact through the control of the resource base. Yet the soils that derive from them have all too often been taken for granted. The soil scientist has come into his own belatedly. Scandinavia at large has relatively poor soils, most of them reflecting the negative effects of latitude. Sands and gravels deposited by the retreating Ice Sheet are widespread. Peat, yielding humus soils for reclamation, is very extensive, especially in the north. Scandinavians have contributed much to the scientific appreciation of peatlands. Only in the south-west of Scandinavia – in the Danish archipelago and Swedish Skåne – are there richer soils comparable with those of central Europe.

Most of the soils claimed by agriculture have been born of water, as has most of the territory occupied by permanent settlement. At large, these soils owe their existence to the emergence of much of Scandinavia from post-glacial seas. Land upheaval, though widespread, has varied greatly in different parts of Scandinavia. In general, it has been least marked in Denmark and most marked in north-central Scandinavia. It is of continuing importance for daily life along the coastlands of Österbotten and Västerbotten. Here land uplift still takes place at the rate of some 80 cms. per century – adding the equivalent of a fair-sized parish every century to the Swedish and Finnish littorals and calling for legal machinery to arrange for the intermittent allocation of the new land. Land upheaval, severing maritime communications between Lake Mälaren and the Baltic Sea, forced the shift of the administrative centre of the Swedish realm to the site that became Stockholm. Ports such as Umeå in Sweden and Pori in Finland have suffered growing problems of access to the sea and have had to construct successive outports. The marine terraces of Norway's fjordland, several hundreds of feet above the present sea level, picturesque as minor hanging gardens of Babylon, give some indication of the scale of land uplift in western Scandinavia.

It is only about 5,000 years since post-glacial seas reached their maximum level. It is less than 10,000 years since the edge of the Quaternary ice cap lay along the lower reaches of Oslofjord, was building the morainic ridge on which Uppsala castle stands and depositing the great ramparts of the Salpausselkä in southern Finland.

As the ice retreated a mantle of vegetation advanced. In the first stages of the rehabilitation Denmark's vegetation was much the same as that of the present-day Lapland fells. Today the Scandinavian countries differ greatly from each other vegetationally. Denmark shares the deciduous woodlands of western Europe, though in Jutland alien plantations of conifers have intruded. Finland and Sweden are the countries of the big woods. Pine on the drier soils and spruce on the damper soils are lightened and brightened by the ubiquitous birch. The same blanket of conifers extends into Norway, though it is less extensive than in Sweden and Finland. As in Iceland, the higher latitudes and higher altitudes of the Scandinavian peninsula have a tundra vegetation, a low flora of creeping and dwarfed habit, in which scrub birch and willow mingle with a variety of berry-bearing plants and gradually yield to mosses, lichens, bald rock and barren scree. The floras of western Europe, of the Arctic and of Eurasia mingle in mainland Scandinavia. The eighteenth-century botanist Linnaeus (Carl von Linné) was nurtured in one of the richest floristic provinces of Sweden. His father's country vicarage in the Scanian parish of Råshult was situated in a virtual Forest of Arden bounded by the serrated skyline of the coniferous north. Its antitheses are found in the forested depths of eastern Finland and in the maritime isolation of Iceland – floristically among the poorest areas in Europe.

The original vegetation of Scandinavia, as that of most of Europe, has been much altered by man. That of Denmark has been changed most widely and most fundamentally. Its landscape is open, with wide vistas of cropped land stretching seaward through the reclaimed marshes of Slesvig to tidal saltmarsh grazings. The landscape of Iceland is also open though for different reasons. The sagas tell of Icelandic woodlands though they probably amounted to little more than groves of scrub birch. Iceland's cultivated land, in total less than one per cent of its area, makes an immediate impact, not only because it is limited, but also because of its colour. In summer the tilled land flashes emerald in a dun-coloured waste. In Sweden and even more in Finland the landscape is as often as not closed, because in most parts woodland takes precedence over cultivated land. In Norway, too, though not with equal intensity in all areas, the original woodland has been denuded for domestic purposes, for industrial and commercial use, by animal grazing in summer, by forest fires and by the impact of disease. The extent and sequence of vegetational change are today revealed by pollen analysis. Meanwhile, conservation has succeeded to exploitation. As forest farming has taken over from natural regeneration, the composition, productivity and ultimately the habitat of the woodlands change. All of these processes have modified and modify increasingly the natural environments of the Scandinavian countries. The changes have been most striking in those areas which the so-called revolutions in transport and industry drew directly into the commercial economy of western Europe without their having passed through any intermediate stages.

The impact upon the fauna has been no less fundamental. Prolonged hunting had already taken its toll of fur-bearing animals by the sixteenth century, so that Europe's fur traders had to look farther afield. But the hardier predators persisted. A century ago travellers to Sweden, Finland and Norway could still witness the ceremonies associated with bear-hunting. Even today the wolf preys upon reindeer herds in the winter and bears make an occasional sortie upon grazing animals; though these are increasingly rare phenomena. A different kind of predator are the seals in the Bothnian archipelagos who, multiplying by the thousand, are the enemies of the fishermen, especially the salmon fishers. Hunters were able to write ecstatically of the feathered life of nineteenth-century Scandinavia. Fishermen found there a paradise of salmon and trout streams. Relatively speaking, wild life remains abundant, but it must be brought increasingly under protective laws. Iceland is least rich in animal life, most of its wild creatures having been brought in by the settlers. However, polar bears may appear along the north coast when hard winters bring the Arctic ice packs farther south.

Around the coastal fringes bird life is rich. Indeed, the bird cliffs of Scandinavia – in the Faeroes and north Norway especially – have not their equal in Europe. But the great birds of prey are rare. Norway has its legendary valleys of eagles. Iceland's order of chivalry is named after the falcon for which it was celebrated in medieval times. Large numbers of Scandinavia's birds are migratory, leaving for kinder climes in the autumn – the storks that build on the cartwheels erected for their rooftop nests in southern Denmark, the swallows and swifts that come for their annual high-latitude feast of mosquitoes and midges, the geese that honk north to summer pastures. Those that overwinter have a range of characteristics, from feeding habits through change of habitat to change of plumage, that enable them to endure low temperatures and snowfall.

Life in the sea no less than life on the land varies regionally. For example, the variety and volume of fish in the Baltic bear no comparison with those in the offshore waters of the outer ocean. Marine life also changes with changing physical and human circumstances. There is still no complete explanation of the shifting seasonal concentrations of herring and cod shoals that so affected the fortunes of Atlantic Scandinavians in earlier times. Nor is there a full understanding of the effects of modern fishing methods upon the rise and fall in fish catches. Suffice to say that fishing protection patrols around territorial waters display a watchfulness unrivalled on the land frontiers of Scandinavia and while Scandinavians may display a benevolent neutrality in international affairs a fishing incident in their territorial waters can provoke a stand-up fight.

As political units each of the countries has a different shape, though there are certain elements common to some if not all of the group. All have an insular or peninsular form. The extreme positions are found in the remote island of Iceland, and in Finland which occupies the Baltic slope of the Fenno-Karelian isthmus. Norway, Sweden and Finland all stretch through six or seven degrees of latitude. Fragmentation of the land area has had fundamental consequences for all five countries. Their coasts, each having its own peculiarities, are for the most part highly dissected. Fragmentation reaches its extreme in the archipelagos of Stockholm, Åland and Turku. Finland's southwestern province of Åland has more than 6,000 islands. The smooth North Sea coast of Jutland, with Europe's longest sand beach between the Skaw and Blaavands Huk, is exceptional.

In a world of islands and peninsulas, movement has naturally been by sea. Historically, indeed, the sea has united and the land has divided – especially where the land bore thick forests, was covered with widespread swamps or rose in precipitous cliffs to extended fells. Within the five countries, between them and beyond them, the sea has served as a natural highway. All Scandinavia looks to the sea and all its member states require freedom of movement upon it. The sea has helped them to find resources throughout the world and, simultaneously, within themselves. Each, too, in its own way has capitalized upon its maritime situation. Not surprisingly, maritime frontiers have generally been more important than land frontiers. The exception is

Finland, whose land boundaries have suffered an instability which contrasts with those of Scandinavia as a whole. The shape of Finland has been very fluid – even its seaward confines were disputed when the political sovereignty of the Åland Islands was challenged in 1920–21.

In addition to basic considerations of latitude, longitude and physical geography, the European setting of the Scandinavian countries must be constantly remembered. The entire area has a measure of detachment from the mainland of Europe, though the degree of detachment varies from country to country. Save when it has been a centre of propulsion or diffusion in its own right, the Scandinavian world has been marginal to the mainstream of European development. For this reason, Finland apart, it also escaped the direct impact of most of Europe's conflicts until the Second World War. At the same time Scandinavia's detachment in the broader European context must not be allowed to obscure the cold facts that, while Sweden and the Danish islands (at least) are central European, Finland is east European. Norway and Jutland (at least) are west European, and Iceland is well on the way to being a part of the New World rather than the Old.

In its narrower North European context, the area can be divided into Baltic Scandinavia and Atlantic Scandinavia. Finland belongs exclusively to Baltic Scandinavia, though from 1918 to 1944 it had direct northern access to the Arctic ocean through the Petsamo corridor. Sweden is predominantly Baltic Scandinavia. Norway, Denmark and Iceland belong to Atlantic Scandinavia. South-western Sweden, facing the Skagerrak and Kattegat, is transitional. So are the Danish islands, clustered at the entrance to what the British used to call (and the Scandinavians still variously call) the Eastsea. The strategic Sound – Öresund to the Scandinavians – has been shared by Denmark and Sweden since the seventeenth century, though Kronborg castle at Elsinore still claimed a shipping toll for Denmark until 1857 and identified the kingdom as the traditional keeper of the Baltic gates. In whichever way they are viewed, these European relationships have given rise to different attitudes in each of the five states. They are inseparable from broader strategic relationships, especially those arising from the historic antithesis between land and sea power.

These facts springing out of location are both supplemented and complemented by the facts of population. The populations of the five countries have a number of common or near-common features. Firstly, four of them have populations small in relation to their surface areas. By contrast, neighbouring big powers on the maritime or continental fronts have large populations (if not necessarily large land areas). This can best be appreciated by comparing their situations with that of Great Britain. Great Britain has a total area of 94,000 sq. mi. (slightly smaller than the state of Oregon) and a population in 1971 of 53·8 millions. Sweden, Norway and Finland are all more extensive than Britain. Their populations are 7.6, 3.7 and 4.6 millions respectively. Iceland, somewhat larger than Ireland, has a population of 200,000. Denmark, with 4.7 millions in its relatively small area, is the only Scandinavian country that approaches the population densities of most European countries.

Secondly, the populations of the Scandinavian countries are ethnically homogeneous. Their territories have not been settled by peoples outside their kith and kin, though there are some peoples outside the political boundaries of Norden who have Scandinavian or Finnish kinship. Because of their isolation and relative poverty in former times, the Scandinavian lands have been areas of emigration rather than immigration; although because of their historical evolution the Scandinavians have spilled over into each other's territories. To a large extent, the peoples of Denmark, Norway and Sweden understand each other's languages. The Icelanders speak a language more closely akin to Old Norse. So do the Faeroese. The Scandinavian countries have no experience of racial minorities. But while four of them have linguistic kinship, Finland is a bilingual country. The Finnish language, in common with Estonian and Hungarian, belongs to the Finno-Ugrian group, and is considered to be a non-Indo-European language. It is as fundamentally different from the Scandinavian languages as it is from Russian. Nearly 92.5 per cent of Finland's inhabitants class themselves as Finnish-speaking. The second language, Swedish, is used by the minority of Finns who occupy principally the south and western coastal areas. There are some 40,000 Lapps widely distributed in the northern quarters of Norway, Sweden and Finland. Their language, rich in dialects, also belongs to the Finno-Ugrian group. Apart from the Danish minority in West German Schleswig (Slesvig to the Danes), the Scandinavians have no irredentisms. A diversity of Finnic peoples, speaking a variety of related languages which greatly attracted the attention of Finnish philologists in the nineteenth century, is found in the USSR; though from the Vepsians in the nearby Karelian borderlands to the Cheremissians in the Urals, they become increasingly archaic.

The great majority of the peoples of Norden adhere nominally to the state church and have followed the Lutheran path since the seventeenth century. The traditions of Lutheranism are more important than the principles and practices, and the church tax is rarely rejected – even by many who cast a Communist vote. Evangelical groups, intermittently firing local enthusiasms, have followings of modest dimensions – none as influential as the pietist wing of the Lutheran church. Finland also has an Orthodox minority of 1.5 per cent. It owes allegiance to Constantinople.

Thirdly, the Scandinavians display certain common demographic characteristics which, in turn, are closely related to the form of social development. Although the birth rate varies considerably from country to country, infant mortality is among the lowest in the world. Life expectancy, high in each country, attains a world record for females in Iceland and males in Sweden. These facts are inseparable from the revolutions in standards of public health and medicine that the Scandinavian countries have enjoyed during the last three generations. It may be an exaggeration to say that the Scandinavian countries have moved from rags to riches in three generations, but it is a fact that they have escaped from the margins of famine to the midst of plenty within living memory. The elimination of dietary deficiencies has both increased resistance to disease and prompted changes in physique. Scandinavians are traditionally tall and blond, but they were less tall in former times. There is ample medical evidence to show how successive generations even in Sweden have added to their stature in the last century. The testimony is still more striking in Finland.

The 22 million Scandinavians are scattered very unevenly over the extensive territories of their homeland. For centuries, the population pushed slowly towards the frontiers of possible settlement, dispersing its energies increasingly thinly over the land. For the contemporary generation, centripetal forces prevail. Cityward migration and urbanization are features as powerful in all the Scandinavian countries as in Western Europe at large. In all of them, too, there are pronounced regional concentrations of population. Each country has a large capital city, though the size is disproportionate in Copenhagen (which claims a quarter of Denmark's population) and Reykjavik (with two-fifths of Iceland's population). None of the five capital cities is centrally located in its national territory. For historical reasons Copenhagen and Stockholm occupy peripheral positions. Helsinki and Oslo are in the extreme south of their latitudinally elongated lands. Reykjavik is in the extreme south-west of Iceland. Beyond this the population of all five countries shows a tendency to concentrate in increasingly restricted areas. Pioneering has not entirely disappeared, but there is widespread retreat from the frontiers of settlement.

Changing population distribution is both a consequence and a cause of the pronounced regional differences in the distribution of industrial and agricultural development in Norden generally – and in Norway, Sweden, Finland and Iceland more particularly. In Norway, Sweden and Finland, there is disparity between their more developed and efficient southern thirds and the less developed and less efficient northern two-thirds. The situation is repeated between Iceland's south-western coastlands and the rest of the island. These regional imbalances are at once good and bad. Since a high degree of industrialization in an economy makes for greater effectiveness and efficiency, and since industry tends to locate near to markets or significant sources of supply, regional disparities are avoidable only by taking social action as a counterweight to economic tendencies. Direct consequences of this situation are, firstly, that the Scandinavian countries tend to juxtapose extensive areas of underdevelopment with intensive areas of development; secondly, that the population minorities of the underdeveloped areas are becoming more conscious of their status and their contributions to the national economies; thirdly, that the central governments divert money both directly and indirectly to the economically under-privileged areas. For Finland, Norway and Sweden these problems reach a climax in their sub-arctic lands – Nordkalotten, as they are called from the Swedish *kalott*, a skull cap; and by extension 'the North Cap'.

The peoples of Norden are increasingly sensitive about the place where they live. For long, they have shown a scientific concern for its physical problems. Against the background of a long-cultivated appreciation of facts and figures, they have come to increasingly precise terms with the resources and opportunities of their somewhat austere world. They have been world leaders in the identification of their lands and the assessment of their resources. For two centuries, men, beasts and crops have been assayed qualitatively as well as quantitatively. The woods are seen more clearly through the trees than in any other part of the world save for Ontario. Standardization of statistics proceeds throughout Norden, while Sweden leads experimentally yet inexorably on to reduce the assessment of its land to a data bank record based on kilometre grid squares. It is the ultimate in quantification and the basis for formal planning of the land. Knowledge provides the key to control. Contemporary Scandinavians certainly display a new control over their environment. For most of them most of the time daily living represents the triumph of people over place; though a minority still remains for whom the art of living still spells that implicitly sensitive relationship between people and place.

2   Origins and development

PEOPLE HAVE OCCUPIED what is today Scandinavia since at least the Quaternary ice sheet retreated from the rocky ribs of coastal Norway and left the low-lying sediments of what was to become Denmark. The Quaternary ice began to expose Scandinavia about 12,000 years ago. The first inhabitants were hunters and fishers – near Eskimo in their culture. Their simple way of life can be reconstructed with increasing accuracy from the artifacts collected by Scandinavian archaeologists and classified into their own particular chronology. Their remains – fish hook, arrow head, precious flint – reflect changing relationships between land and sea and the changing climates that played upon them. Their magic art, chiselled in rock drawings of which hundreds have been lovingly restored, reveals their primitive practices.

Once a rudimentary agriculture was practised and the hunters and fishers became settled, they explored the opportunities offered by the maritime foreland and by the forested and mountainous hinterlands. Expanding populations reclaimed the former and colonized the latter. Displays in Scandinavian museums often rivet attention to these earlier settlers. Tromsö museum fixes the bleak Stone Age culture of North Norway firmly in the eye: the doors of Helsinki's national museum open on to the comb ceramic pots that remain from the days when peninsular Finland was still an archipelago enjoying a kinder climate than today.

While burial mounds on the modest eminences of Denmark or the plains of southern Sweden may claim some attention from the traveller, the richer discoveries from earlier times derive from more obscure sites. Above all it is in the peat bogs that some of the oldest and most remarkable relics have been preserved. Skis, dated by carbon analysis as six to seven thousand years old, have been recovered from peat bogs in northern Sweden and Finland. The bog people of Denmark are more a feature of local lore than those of Ireland; while Denmark's two-thousand-year-old Bronze Age relics include human remains, the best features of which rival those of Egyptian mummies. Certainly no Nilotic tomb has yielded a head which in the quality of its preservation equals that of Tollund man (Pl. 1; in Silkeborg museum in Denmark), though the workmanship of early northern goldsmiths – as suggested by the sun image from Trundholm in north Zealand – was inferior to that of Mediterranean craftsmen from comparable periods. Both bogs and drifting sand (as at Lindholm in north Jutland) have also preserved the equipment of those who lived through bleaker days than the sun-worshipping Bronze Age people. The harness and accoutrements of cavalrymen mingle with objects imported or pillaged from the outposts of the superior material cultures to the south. In bogs, too, and in the silt of former harbours, have been preserved the oldest relics of Scandinavian ships. Roskilde fjord in Denmark has yielded specimens that anticipate the Viking type vessels associated with ship burials in Funen's Ladby or the ceremonial Oseberg ship from Tönsberg in south Norway.

The earlier inhabitants of Scandinavia left few impressive monuments on the face of the land. Stone had been piled upon stone with some lasting effect in Dark Age and Viking strongholds, but the mason has only played a role during the last millennium. In Trelleborg on Zealand, the Danes have restored a fortified settlement site from the early Viking period. Norway, Sweden and Finland have their hill forts, though in common with ship burial sites they have been generally obscured by the forest mantle. Such features, increasingly protected as public monuments, add to the Viking legend and the disproportionate part that it plays in historical texts dealing with Scandinavia.

Already by the Viking era, the peoples of Scandinavia had been identified. They were Norsemen who spoke a nearly common tongue and whose bases were principally the inlets around the Skagerrak and Kattegat. Their legendary summer raiding obscures other equally important aspects of their overseas movement. The Viking period was simultaneously an age of exploration both eastwards and westwards. In the east Norse movement along the water courses coupled with settlement led to the formation of a Russian state. In the west there were successive climaxes in the settlement of Iceland, the colonization of Greenland and the Vinland landfalls in Newfoundland–Labrador. More peaceful emigration from home territories, which in many cases suffered population pressure, also brought substantial Scandinavian settlement to the British Isles.

The Viking episode was important for Scandinavia for two other reasons – firstly, its achievements were rooted in improved social organization, and secondly, they were inseparable from the stimulus of intensified outside contacts. Although the Viking forays were bent upon pillage, they could scarcely help bringing in their train new ideas, techniques and equipment to the barbaric marchlands of northern Europe. The process may have been slow, but it was cumulative over a span of years equal to that separating the mid-eighteenth century and the present day.

The introduction of Christianity was among the consequences of increased contacts. The first missionary journeys into Scandinavia were made by Bishop Ansgar as early as AD 826. Possibly the farthest point of his journey was the island of Birka in Lake Mälaren, where one of the earliest concentrations of settlement in Sweden was located. Harald Bluetooth, recalled in the legend on an impressive runic stone at Jelling in central Jutland, first 'made the Danes Christians'. King Olaf's triumph over the pagan forces at Stiklestad in 1030 represented a turning point in the history of Norway. As a result Olaf became the patron saint of his country and his feast day (Olsok) on 29 July continues to be celebrated by both the church militant and pagan bonfires. As was common in the Roman Catholic conversion, ecclesiastical monuments were grafted on to pagan sites. In Sweden the giant tumuli at old Uppsala traditionally identified as the burial mounds of sixth-century monarchs were complemented by the cathedral at new Uppsala on the then navigable Fyris river. To the east Swedish twelfth-century crusades to south-western Finland had a dual motive – conversion and resistance to the slow Orthodox penetration from the south-east, a penetration which was to leave to Finland a permanent legacy of Russian (and subsequently Greek) Orthodox adherents. To the west Christianity was brought to Iceland in AD 1000, and a bishopric was established at Gardar in west Greenland, the church foundations of which are preserved to this day. But pagan practices were slow to disappear in the North. Fell, forest, swamp and the sheer distance between places of worship diminished the authority of the priesthood. The old gods lived on beside the new. Indeed, magic rites and a whiff of witchcraft have lingered into the twentieth century – not only among the Lapps. In addition, the necromancy attributed to the Finnmarkers and transferred to the Finns was to be enshrined in the literature of the sea from Henry Dana, through Joseph Conrad to C. S. Forester.

In its outward forms no less than in its inner spirit, the Roman church in Scandinavia was at once militant and compliant. It was compliant in its architecture, absorbing characteristics of Viking art. The infinitely intertwined patterns that decorate the carved doors and lintels of Norwegian churches (Pl. 18) such as those at Lom and Urnes are a direct extension of the animalistic designs that embellish the handles of Viking swords. Such wooden stave churches with their scaly brown pagoda-like roofs repeat in their dragon motifs the prows of Viking ships. On the exposed Baltic front of Scandinavia, church and military outpost were sometimes one. Here stone prevailed over wood as the building material. The rounded fortress church of St Ols on Denmark's island of Bornholm and the fortified churches in Sweden's outlying island of Gotland are representative. In general the earliest stone-built churches had Gothic features. Though glass was a precious commodity and windows were small, wall paintings soon ran riot over the spacious walls (to be restored to their medieval glory five hundred years later), while woodcarvers produced their Gothic altar figures and crucifixes. In Finland the chapels of the Orthodox parishes, built of wood and subject to the risk of fire and decay, rarely survived as architectural monuments; but the monastery of Valamo on an island in Lake Ladoga remained a colourful showplace in pre-war Finland.

Scandinavian saints and martyrs emerged with expanding Christianity. In Finland an English bishop, Henry, was the first martyr and his successor, Thomas, the first historically identifiable bishop. Other holy people left their shrines, among them none more influential than St Birgitta in Sweden. Simultaneously the religious houses introduced new practices to northern agriculture and provided a new stimulus to trading. The Cistercians in western Norway brought crops and stocks from their parent homes in the Yorkshire dales to such places as Lysekloster (south of Bergen) and Munkholm (in north Tröndelag). On the western marchlands of their territory the eastern church pursued a similar course in what was to become Finnish Karelia. The apple tree was probably introduced at much the same time from both east and west. Trade was carried in vessels belonging to the religious orders as well as in ordinary merchantmen.

The church introduced an organization into Scandinavia which at once underlined and complemented that of the emerging kingdoms. Although the Scandinavian countries knew no fully-developed feudal system as in mainland Europe, they experienced varying degrees of it. A military hierarchy developed, the unit of local government or *herred* deriving its name from the smallest territory responsible for mustering a prescribed number of mounted soldiers: the hundred, for a unit mustering 100–120 men. Although fortresses were few and far between, they had already begun to appear by the twelfth century. Of some, such as King Valdemar's castle at Ribe in Danish Slesvig, nothing remains but the grassy mound on which the keep stood. Their design owed much to mainland Europe. Sweden's former outposts at Kastelholm and Turku display evidence that their masons were familiar with constructional methods known in France. Merchant fraternities and trading fellowships came into being at the same time.

Organization and administration called for systems of taxation by both spiritual and lay powers. Taxation was closely tied to land at an early stage – the ultimate consequence has been the elaborate qualitative assessment of land for present-day taxation purposes. Both the form and character of cultivation and the form and character of ownership differed regionally. So, too, did inheritance. Field systems differentiated the landscape and left their varied imprints. Axel Steensburg's use of air photography and field analysis to reconstruct the system of the settlement of Borup Ris in Jutland (*c.* 1000–1200) provides a precise illustration of an earlier cultivation pattern. Continuity of a different character is found in the Odal law of Norway, a land inheritance provision which (also lingering in the Faeroes) distinguishes Norway from the rest of Scandinavia. Early concern with land tax and land law has yielded its own harvest of documents to complement the manuscripts of sacred texts, of treaties and of sagas. The words employed in these documents reflect the role of church and state in fostering the use of Latin; but the runic script lingered into the Christian era. It was employed, for example, on medieval Icelandic gravestones. In Iceland the vernacular never entirely yielded to Latin in church worship.

Eastwards, the culture of western Europe encountered that of emerging Muscovy. Swedish crusades pushed through Finland to the Karelian isthmus where the religious and military outpost of Viborg was established by Tyrgils Knutsson in 1293. The province of Karelia, focusing upon Lake Ladoga, was to remain one of Europe's fatefully disputed territories.

Medieval Finland, an appendage of Sweden, was administered from Stockholm after the thirteenth century. By then the Svear and Götar peoples were united and their capital had been shifted sea-wards as Mälaren was transformed from an arm of the sea into a lake by the slow uplift of the land. By this time too, colonists from among the Finns, concentrated in the south-western interior province of Häme (called Tavastland by the Swedes) and the south-eastern province of Karelia, had penetrated inland to Savo (Sw. Savolax). The Finns, westernmost of the widely dispersed Finno-Ugrian peoples, followed a pastoral and hunting existence. The essentials of it may be gleaned from *Kalevala*, their oral poetry collected and arranged by Elias Lönnrot in the early nineteenth century. As the Finns expanded northwards, the Lapps retreated before them, leaving a legacy of place-names to mark their former reindeer pastures. Similarly, place-names offer clues to the process of settlement in the dales of eastern Norway (a process immortalized by Sigrid Undset in her epic novel *Kristin Lavransdatter*) and the interior valleys of Sweden. It is appropriate that at a later stage in history the hearth of European place-name studies should be established at the University of Lund where, under the leadership of Eilert Ekwall, a more scientific inter-pretation was initiated during the early years of the twentieth century.

While mainland Scandinavians were wresting cropland from the forest with fire and axe, the island Scandinavians were establishing themselves on the exposed wastes of the Atlantic islands. Here fisher-farming complemented the forest-farming of eastern Scandinavia. Literature bloomed earlier in the western isles than among the eastern woods. It was not only the feeling for words that marked the great leap forward, but the ability of some of the storytellers or learned men to commit them to durable parchment. Saga and edda, the product of Iceland's literary golden age (1200–1350), may seem to focus on bloody feuds and mythical heroes, but they also contain much about the detail of economy and society. George Dasent sub-titled his translation of *Burnt Njal's Saga*, 'Life in Iceland at the end of the tenth century'. Accounts of the recovery of the manuscripts are often as remarkable as the literature is exciting. *Flateyjarbók*, written by two Icelandic priests and dated 1387–94, was found on the island of Flatey in the seventeenth century. It contains the sagas of the Norse kings – including that of St Olaf himself. Volumes such as the *Codex Regius* of the older edda, humble in appearance, are the source of heroic poems such as the prophetic *Völuspa* and *Havamál*.

As systems of government formalized, law was also committed in more permanent form to vellum. Where the Norse went they established their meeting or *Thing* places. None of them approached the classical democratic assembly more closely than that held in the natural lava amphitheatre of Iceland's Thingvellir. Here, after AD 930, descendants of the original settlers listed in the *Book of Land Taking* (Landnámabók) participated in the annual summer gathering.

The record and practice of the law differed from country to country. By the thirteenth century, for example, Denmark had established three separate areas of jurisdiction. They were Jutland, Sjælland and Skåne, and each had its separate law books. The creation of a unitary code out of its regional laws was a measure of the integration of the nation. And the halo of divinity that hedged the king was transmitted to the book of laws that bore his name. Magnus Eriksson's early Swedish Law Book and Christian V's Law Book of Denmark and Norway represented climaxes in the codification of the laws of Baltic Scandinavia and Atlantic Scandinavia respectively.

While the sun cast fitful shafts of light over medieval Scandinavia, the fifteenth century spelt the onset of afflictions both to the body and the soul. Their origins were partly physical. Worsening of the climate had a direct effect upon the meagre harvests of high-latitude Europe, bringing hunger and famine in train. At the same time increased storminess added hazards to communications by sea. The links with Greenland were severed and the Norse colony in it succumbed. While climatic deterioration was fundamental, the reason for the final extinction of the settlement remains a mystery. In Iceland the advance of ice to the north shore reduced the harvest from the sea as well as from the land. The Black Death added to the toll of winter's white death. To its effects are ascribed many features of the decline of the North – from deserted settlement sites to diminished trade, from the weakened control of legal and ecclesiastical authority to the shifts in power out of which the new arrangement of the Scandinavian states was born.

At the end of the Middle Ages the Scandinavian world drew together in a dynastic union under Erik of Pomerania, whose realm anticipated the ideal of the twentieth-century Nordic Council. The division of the north into Atlantic and Baltic Scandinavia following the accession of Queen Margaret in 1388 foreshadowed the course of Nordic history for the next three centuries. Denmark and Norway, with outlying Iceland, remained under a common crown until 1814. Sweden, with its eastern wing Finland, remained a unitary state until 1809. Much to the relief of other European countries, antipathies developed between the two halves. Baltic and Atlantic Scandinavia were locked in intermittent struggles until the eventual triumph of Sweden at the end of the war of 1657–60. By the ensuing peace Sweden finally achieved 'peninsular completeness', taking over the provinces of Skåne, Halland and Blekinge from Denmark. Copenhagen was left excentric to Denmark on the shores of a divided Sound, though it continued to extract dues from ships passing through the channel at Elsinore. Lund, now a Swedish city, acquired a bishopric and a university, both intended to combat the lingering Danish allegiance. Three centuries later Scanians still retain a distinctly Danish accent, while developments around the Sound confirm the continuing pull of Copenhagen.

Although there were dynastic divisions and political conflicts between Atlantic and Baltic Scandinavia, the Reformation provided a potentially unifying force. The Reformation, beginning as a genuinely religious protest, was rapidly enlisted to support monarchical ambitions and to buttress the philosophy of the nation state. Among the monarchs Gustavus Vasa of Sweden was outstanding. In the same years and with the same results as Henry VIII in England, he confiscated the possessions of the church, assumed its titular headship and founded a dynasty of European stature. In the process Sweden also escaped from the commercial control of the Hanseatic cities. Although Denmark had its share of civil bloodshed during the early sixteenth-century conflict between the aristocracy and the monarchy, the Reformation passed without serious problems, with Christian IV an established head of the church by the new century. The successful adoption of Lutheranism in the North is inseparable from the gradualist policies of some of its outstanding churchmen. Finland, for example, was fortunate in having Michael Agricola, a moderate bishop who believed more in the persuasive value of education than in a downright assault on the old practices and rites. Iceland passed peacefully over to the new faith. Its last Roman Catholic bishop died in 1550, and the first Lutheran bishops brought with them their own hymn books. Iceland's first hymnal – *Psalmabók* – is dated 1589.

Nevertheless, the fabric of the Scandinavian churches and religious foundations suffered material damage. The colourful wall-paintings were blotted out; church furnishings were removed; vestments yielded to sober black. Latin was replaced by the vernacular, choirs were succeeded by cantors, new concepts of discipline were imposed, new forms of intolerance emerged (witch-hunting darkened Scandinavia no less than Puritan England and its North American colonies), new burdens of guilt were accumulated.

Although the Scandinavian world suffered fratricidal disputes, the great release of energy accompanying the Reformation was also directed beyond the seas. At the climax of its powers, in the latter half of the seventeenth century, Sweden bestrode the narrow Baltic like a Colossus, while under its Protestant leadership the rump of Europe was racked with the Thirty Years' War. Gustavus Adolphus established his place in history and Sweden's yellow and blue flag acquired the familiarity of the red and white Danish banner. Sweden was too busily involved in mainland Europe to sustain an overseas empire, so that its colonies on the Delaware fell to Britain. Denmark, with trading stations established in three continents, never capitalized upon them and eventually sold its scatter of tropical islands and territorial enclaves. The Age of the Reformation brought a new political security to the North, but it was a security under autocracy. The form of despotism differed in Atlantic and Baltic Scandinavia. In Denmark, a balance was usually struck between aristocracy and burghers. In Sweden the monarchy worked more closely with the aristocracy, whose castles and manor houses complemented the royal palaces. The baroque and rococo showpieces that they built are usually national monuments today. Sometimes they are still occupied by families whose ancestors created them. And although historic titles are employed less publicly than privately, noblemen's calendars linger on in Denmark, Finland and Sweden to add a piquant note to their proverbially democratic societies. The age of the Baroque also bequeathed ecclesiastical monuments – modest perhaps by Central European standards, but of the same lineage. Ornament, colour and gilt crept back into churches – nowhere more lavishly than in

Denmark's Frederiksborg chapel. Men were puffed up sartorially and monarchy (as represented, for example, by Christian IV of Denmark or Gustavus Adolphus, Queen Christina and Charles XII of Sweden) was of more than life-size stature. The accoutrements and armour of war were woven into artistic motifs, the pageantry of the court was recorded on copper plates, portraiture developed, the mapmaker engraved a record of the realms.

The reaction of the North to the Renaissance is well illustrated in contemporary Scandinavian museums; but little remains of the contribution of the anonymous peasantry. Yet the peasant was absolutely dominant, however low the key in which his life was pitched. Most Scandinavians lived close to the earth; in Iceland's sod houses, literally *in* the earth. The open-field husbandry around the thatched wattle-and-daub homes of Denmark's compact villages, the sheep on what a medieval churchman called 'the howling wilderness' of the heath and the meagre cattle migrant on trails to the lush salt marshes resembled the pattern of western Europe more closely than that of the rest of Scandinavia. The lineaments of the subsistence economy that prevailed over most of Norway, Sweden and Finland until the mid-nineteenth century were well-established. The high noon of this economy – with its usually isolated farmstead, frequently extended family, limited infield, extensive open-range animal husbandry, hunting and fishing rights – was the background to Harriet Martineau's romance, *Feats on the Fiord*. Only along the coasts and over limited areas was a full exchange economy practised. Mineral workings or iron ore dredgings (from the lakes) and smelting with the aid of charcoal furnaces and water-driven hammers promoted some local trading. Along the coasts softwood timber was harvested for constructional work, sawmills multiplied, naval stores were assembled from the pitch and tar burneries, the scattered oak groves were denuded for men-of-war (only the luckless *Vasa*, raised from the mud of Stockholm harbour and preserved in a museum, remains). Essentials – above all salt, cheese, preserved meat, frozen game and dried fish – moved to markets traditionally held in winter when the sleigh speeded transport. The British artist John Atkinson painted them in Finland; the traveller Edward Clark described them.

Paradoxically it was Scandinavia in retreat that became aware of the need for a fuller assessment and more careful utilization of its resources. The defeat of Charles XII at Poltava in 1709 and the establishment by Russia of St Petersburg as its new capital foreshadowed a century of pressure on Sweden's eastern border. The Great Northern War terminated in 1721, hostilities broke out again in 1743–5, in 1789–90 and culminated with the loss of Finland to Russia in 1809. Paradoxically it was Scandinavia in a state of domestic stress – both political and economic – which assembled some of the most valuable information about the resources of the Nordic countries. Population censuses were initiated (so that Sweden and Finland have a continuous series of demographic records since about 1750), comparative crop yields and animal numbers were collected, detailed military map-making and coastal surveys were set in motion. More importantly, land reorganization laws were passed with a view to replacing fragmented holdings by unitary farmsteads. Sweden – Finland led the way in 1747; Denmark followed with a more rigorous programme in the 1790s.

Side by side with the rise of political arithmetic ran a growing curiosity about the world of nature. It was part of a European movement, but the North gave impetus to it. It found expression in *Wunderkammer* such as that of Ole Worm in Copenhagen – a progenitor of contemporary Scandinavia's splendid museums. It gave birth to scientific societies such as the Swedish Academy of Sciences (1739), the principal objectives of which were practical and applied. Purposeful topographic journeys were undertaken in Norway, Sweden and Finland by naturalists – best known of which was the widely translated *Lapland Journey* (1737) of Carolus Linnaeus. Linnaeus, a typical eighteenth-century polymath, sent disciples from Uppsala to the five continents to discover new plants for his homeland. Worship of nature was also expressed in magnificent books such as *Flora Danica* (the publication of which was spread over 1761–83, and inspired, in name and design, the best-known patterns of Danish porcelain).

Simultaneously, the Scandinavians sought from Britain, France, the Netherlands and the north German principalities, new crops, stock, methods of cultivation, and farm equipment to improve their retarded agriculture. Frogner Park in Oslo, home of Bernt Anker (1746–1805), was a centre of diffusion for the new farm practices. By the end of the eighteenth century the Scandinavians had created their own agricultural and economic societies to promote the new husbandry, to establish new industry and to urge commercial reform. Workshops multiplied – ceramics, for example, in Copenhagen and Rörstrand in Sweden, glass in Småland.

The slow ferment that was affecting husbandman and craftsman, entrepreneur and merchant received scant attention in the diplomatic dispatches of ministers because domestic political squabbles and the court intrigues of Copenhagen and Stockholm appeared to be of greater import. Internationally, eighteenth-century Denmark and Sweden followed different courses – autocratic Denmark aspiring to neutrality, Sweden, in the so-called *Age of Liberty* (1718–72), assailed by land and sea on its eastern front. Court life in the Northern capitals aped that of France. If it drained national exchequers by the construction of such extravagances as the Swedish summer palace of Drottningholm, it bequeathed proud pleasure domes to posterity. It also brought patronage of the arts. In Sweden, the age of Gustavus III (1746–92) is summed up in the artistic achievements of C. G. Tessin. In Denmark, the aristocracy sought to have themselves painted in the leafy settings of their estates; Cornelius Høyer to reduce them to miniature ivories; printers and binders to produce works of art for their libraries. Meanwhile Carl Michael Bellman, ballad-maker of the age, left a legacy of song to the North not rivalled even by that of John Gay's *Beggars' Opera;* while through student societies such as *Det Norske Selskab* (The Norwegian Society) literary fashions from England and France were introduced.

The Napoleonic period witnessed primary shifts in the allegiances and interests of the North. Blockade and counter-blockade disturbed established patterns of trading. Denmark and Sweden became increasingly aware of their declining military status and of the rise of greater European powers in whose system of equilibrium they were suspended. The changes and chances brought a British fleet to bombard Copenhagen in 1807 and the convoy of Sir John Moore with 10,000 men to Gothenburg to sustain Sweden in 1808; a retinue headed by a Napoleonic general who ascended the tottering throne of Sweden in 1810 to establish the House of Bernadotte; and a Russian tsar, Alexander I, to Borgå Cathedral in 1809 to receive the personal fealty of Finland. Politically – and in some respects economically as well – it was the end of an era.

3   The shaping of modern Scandinavia

IN 1815 THE CONGRESS of Vienna confirmed the transfer of the Grand
Duchy of Finland from Sweden to Russia and the establishment of
the dual monarchy of Sweden–Norway arranged by the Treaty of
Kiel in the preceding year. Under the terms of the treaty, Iceland, the
Faeroe Islands and Greenland remained dependent territories of
Denmark. Since the twelfth century Finland had been the eastern
half of the Swedish realm: since the middle of the fifteenth century
Norway had been united under a common monarch with Denmark.

By the time that these political adjustments were agreed it was
already evident that the Scandinavian states were failing both technically and economically to keep abreast of the European pacemakers. Bankruptcy is a word employed regularly in Scandinavian
historical texts to describe the financial situation of the countries of
Norden as the industrial and commercial revolutions broke upon
western Europe. The Scandinavian countries lacked money to purchase capital goods, entrepreneurs to mobilize them, technicians to
operate them, domestic markets to consume their products, and
overseas possessions to add economies of scale. Furthermore, because
of these shortcomings, Scandinavia became increasingly a tributary
territory of the new industrialized states which were hungry for its
raw materials. Experienced entrepreneurs of Britain, Germany,
France and the Low Countries seized upon its potentialities. The
multiplication of trading links was reflected in the growth of hon-
orary consuls in the ports of Scandinavia. No less important were the
widely varied west European enterprises established in Scandinavia
itself. Mining concerns sought out sites along the Norwegian coast
(such as Dunderland and Sulitjelma) and in the depths of the Finnish
lake district (such as Joroinen and Pitkaranta) before eventually aspiring to the greater prizes of Sweden's Lapland sites. Timber merchants

multiplied steam mills so that by the 1870s, a Swedish wit could write of the Sundsvall area, 'Saw by saw I saw, nor else I saw'. Textile manufacturers acquired the power rights of falls such as Tammerkoski in south-west Finland. Following the tradition of much Scandinavian workshop industry, the new plants also displayed an element of paternalism in their management. They were country-based rather than town-based, offered new if localized opportunities and helped to reduce rural employment. Yet idyllic though most Scandinavian industrial sites might appear by comparison with those of urbanized western Europe, they were frequently set in areas of rural stagnation with all their attendant physical and mental afflictions. As early as the 1830s the Swedish historian E. G. Geijer was urging the importance of studying poverty as well as wealth. Peace, potatoes and vaccination aided population increase, but did little to reduce indigence.

The rise of trading and industry was inseparable from improved transport. Steamships multiplied the number of journeys in a given time as well as extending the trading season. By the 1830s the throb of their engines was a sound established in Scandinavian waters. The size of ships grew as steel plating replaced timber, though the mercantile marines of the north still included wooden sailing vessels well into the twentieth century. The Ålanders kept sailing vessels on the Australian grain run until 1939. Railways slowly spread their thin networks – beginning in Denmark in the 1840s, eventually arriving in Finland (where the Russian gauge was employed) in the 1860s. From the outset railways were primarily state-sponsored and many of the engineers who constructed them came from Great Britain.

A new concern for measurement and exactness accompanied the machines and instruments that invaded Scandinavia. Country folk who had long responded to the shadows cast by the sun on mountain flank and copper dial were regulated first by the clock (a richly encased possession of most families) and then by the timetables of steamships and railways. Their traditional units of measurement were officially replaced by the metric system in the last quarter of the nineteenth century, but local references to them die hard. Organization of money as well as time engaged attention. Modern Scandinavian banking has its roots in the 1860s and 1870s.

The steel needed for the new means of transport fell sharply in price following the introduction of the large-scale Bessemer converter after 1860. In turn, cheaper transport hastened the impact of other technical discoveries on the Scandinavian countries. Two were of paramount importance – the Gilchrist-Thomas process for refining phosphoric ores in steel production and the mechanical and chemical means of producing paper from softwood timber. Both belonged to the 1870s. Following in the wake of their adoption came the electric generator. Finland, Norway and Sweden benefited greatly from all three of these discoveries – Sweden most of all. Scandinavia conceived its own inventive geniuses – both theoretical and applied. They included Denmark's H. C. Ørsted who changed the concept of electromagnetism in a modest paper published in Latin in 1820; the taciturn Swede Alfred Nobel, the peaceful uses of whose explosive energy were to be subordinated to those of war; the mechanically ingenious C. G. P. de Laval, whose invention of a cream separator changed the character of dairying; the Norwegian chemist Samuel Eide, whose experiments resulted in the immense nitrate industry now but part of the ramifications of *Norsk Hydro;* S. Wingquist, who created the ball-bearing industry, and L. M. Ericsson, who was Europe's answer to the telephones of Edison and Bell.

While each technical discovery in the international field had its own chain of reactions in the countries of Norden, each European movement developed its own particular Scandinavian expression. Romanticism for example released a flood of literature – from the poems of Henrik Wergeland in Norway and J. L. Runeberg in Finland, to the romances of Steen Steensen Blicher in Denmark and P. D. A. Atterbom in Sweden. Nationalism, closely related to the romantic movement, evoked markedly differing responses in each country. It was doubly powerful in semi-autonomous Finland, which was seeking both political independence of Russia and cultural independence of Sweden and the Swedish language. The encouragement of the Finnish language as an instrument of expression was central to the rise of nationhood. In Norway national feeling was also fostered through the arts, and a new literary language (*landsmål*) came into being in antithesis to the official language (*riksmål*) of the government. Ripples in the currents of liberalism that flowed through Europe also had their Scandinavian expressions. In Denmark, for example, autocratic monarchy ended with the new constitution of 1849 and its associated reforms. Scandinavianism also emerged as a movement in its own right. Support for it was most vocal during the Prussian assault on Denmark in 1864. Romanticism, nationalism, liberalism, and Scandinavianism all drew their succour from an educated minority. For mental and technical enlightenment the Scandinavians were not slow to realize the need for a literate – and numerate – majority.

Yet literacy and numeracy were only one side of life and the success of Scandinavian education is inseparable from other considerations. They included the folk high school movement which, under Bishop Grundtvig's guidance, blended the practical, the national and the religious in its approach to education; the technical high schools, founded in the capital cities, that drew their inspiration primarily from those of Germany; the new cult of physical education that owed much to P. A. Ling's gymnastic methods and A. E. Nordenskiöld's promotion of winter sports; and the vocational institutions, such as the forestry schools, that looked to the scientific exploitation of resources.

Scandinavians were forced to adjust themselves to situations developing across the oceans as well as across their narrower home seas. Few events in the recent history of the Scandinavian countries have been more important than large-scale emigration to the New World. Each of the Nordic countries experienced the full consequences of emigration, though the climax differed from country to country in time. It exceeded 30,000 a year for Sweden during some years in the 1880s. The reaction was delayed in Finland and Iceland until the turn of the century. Emigration was from rural Scandinavia to rural America, and it yielded a great legacy of imaginative literature as well as of autobiography. The fever was cured at least as much by domestic improvements and inducements as by American restraints. Meanwhile it had side effects. They included the rise of the English language as a rival to the German language in Scandinavia and the establishment of the Norwegian-American and Swedish-American Lines to serve the emigrants on the North Atlantic run.

The occupation of the western lands of North America had an additional consequence for Denmark. The revolution in its agriculture was hastened if not precipitated by the flood of cheap grain exported from the New World to Europe. Danish farmers had to find a new role. As purveyors to the West European breakfast table, they may be deemed to have displayed all of the qualities of self-help that Samuel Smiles recommended. Swedish farming, affected in the same manner but not to the same degree, was given protection – which, in turn, intensified differences between the agricultural and industrial parties.

Economic change stirred social change. As they struggled for a vision of the new affluence, Scandinavians became conscious of the shortcomings of their several societies. There were varied reactions. Spiritual responses followed neither Emanuel Swedenborg's mysticism nor Søren Kierkegaard's intellectualism, but inclined either to the pietist or to the evangelical form. Among pietist groups, the followers of L. L. Læstadius claimed particular attention because of the missionary appeal of their movement to the Lapps and their high-latitude neighbours. The impact of free church movements, deriving their inspiration from those of Britain, was more local than national. In the towns the Salvation Army raised its battle cry, though the conditions that called it into being no longer exist. The familiar psalm books of the present-day Lutheran church were assembled, drawing on the abundant poetic inspiration of the time for new hymns. Inseparable from spiritual revival and the sharpening of the social conscience was the rise of temperance movements. They acquired a sufficiently powerful support for all of the countries save Denmark to impose restraints upon the production and distribution of alcohol. Finland pushed temperance to its limits in the unsuccessful prohibition experiment of 1919–31.

The exaggerated attitudes adopted towards alcohol are matched by an almost pathological concern for cleanliness – a concern probably related to the early recognition of hygienic shortcomings in Scandinavia's potentially wealthy communities. Maldistribution of wealth is a relative term and, by comparison with the gap between rich and poor in most European countries, that in Scandinavia has always been modest. Yet a rural proletariat remained in all the Nordic countries after poverty had been eliminated from the towns. The battle of the Scandinavians against undernourishment, infant mortality and killing diseases such as tuberculosis was conducted with growing intensity as they entered into their new financial heritage. It is a far cry from the tubercular poets of nineteenth- and early twentieth-century Scandinavia, through the architectural triumphs of inter-war sanatoria, to the deserted wards of the post-war years.

The impulse to change was felt in all areas of activity – literary, industrial and governmental. In literary circles, figures of European stature challenged established values. In Denmark Georg Brandes ploughed a libertarian furrow before Henrik Ibsen sought to 'torpedo the ark' in Norway and August Strindberg exposed in his autobiographical *Son of a Servant* the social unrest of the Sweden of his youth. The tradition that they established was followed by a school of socially conscious authors. The plight of the underprivileged in outwardly idyllic Oslo stirred Hans Jaeger as that of the outcasts on the highways and byways of the countryside was to move Knut Hamsun. The Swedish urban proletariat found a sympathetic response in Martin Koch; those who occupied the back alleys of Copenhagen, in M. A. Nexø; the Finns who starved in the slums of Kotka's timber town, in Toivo Pekkanen. The tradition was to be continued in Iceland by Halldor Laxness. The parallel rise of the popular press (promising centennials and jubilees for a considerable number of familiar newspapers in the later twentieth century) provided another outlet for the expression of public opinion.

On the industrial front, trade unions were already concentrating their activities in central organizations by 1900, though their scale of operations was limited by comparison with that of countries such as Britain or Germany. In the earlier stages of their development they responded freely to external influences. In their maturity, they were to forget the unsavoury and violent episodes of their youth, and to attain agreed codes of conduct which were to make them some of the most effective in the world.

The rise of the unions was inseparable from the growth of radical groups, most important of which were the Social-Democratic and Labour parties that were born in the 1880s. In all countries except Iceland they were to become at one stage or another the most powerful political party, though in the process they shed their more radical qualities. Their development differed from country to country. In Sweden and Denmark they gained political representation in the 1890s: in Finland and Norway during the following decade. Domestic politics were complicated by the struggle for constitutional independence in both Norway and Finland. In the former, escape from the union with Sweden remained the central political issue until peaceful separation was arranged in 1905. In the latter, the antipathy between Finnish-speaking and Swedish-speaking Finns modified divisions along the usual progressive and conservative party lines. After 1899, when Russian pressure on Finland increased, internal politics were also split between those who were actively anti-Russian and those who adopted a conciliatory attitude. Activists came to be associated with revolutionaries. Indeed, because of their geography, the Scandinavian countries in general and Sweden and Finland in particular provided routeways for what has been called a 'northern underground' of emissaries and exiles whose purpose was the overthrow of the tsarist régime. In its earlier stages radical thinking in Scandinavia was more often Marxist than humanist. It was also much more articulate than in many countries and has remained so. Furthermore, the progressive elements had a strong feminine component. Left-wing patriotism was partly responsible for the political enfranchisement of women earlier in Finland and Norway than anywhere else in Europe. The Scandinavian countries as a whole were among the first in Europe to achieve universal suffrage; though their women were to discover that there was more to liberation than a vote, a seat in parliament or entry to the professions. Elements of the patriarchal society still persist towards the margins of settlement even in the Nordic countries.

Monarchy contrived to maintain its position in spite of political and social changes. When Norway became independent it elected for a monarchy and a Danish prince restored a line of Haakons, Olavs and Haralds to the throne. Only the defeat of Germany prevented independent Finland from having the brother-in-law of Kaiser Wilhelm II of Germany as its king. The abolition of the monarchy was a feature of Sweden's Social-Democratic programme at an early stage in the history of the party, but the Bernadotte family still occupies the throne.

Scandinavian industry was struck by political and social change at a different stage in its evolution from that in the older industrial countries. As a result the Nordic countries were saved from many of the urban problems suffered elsewhere. Furthermore, political changes began to assert themselves at a favourable juncture in their economic circumstance. In the years immediately before the First World War the Scandinavians had something to sell in a world wanting to buy it at the same time as they sought to obtain capital in a world anxious to lend it. But their dependence upon a vigorous external trade placed them in a vulnerable situation in a militarily divided Europe. Sweden found itself divided on its external allegiances, as well as domestically riven between the militarists and the anti-militarists. Following the outbreak of the First World War the Scandinavian countries took immediate steps to maintain their neutrality. The war years were hard for them all. As maritime nations they suffered heavy shipping losses, independently of the disruption of their vital trade. Food and fuel shortages led to famine conditions. Sympathies were divided between the Allies and the Central Powers, making for further cleavages. The problem was heightened in Finland by the Civil War, where the White army led by General Mannerheim could hardly have gained power without at least indirect support from Germany. This assistance at a critical stage in its national life established a bond between Finland and Germany which was to be remembered in a variety of ways in the following generation.

Nor did the Versailles Peace bring immediate harmony to the North. In Baltic Scandinavia the instabilities of the Russian situation were transmitted to Finland, whose eastern borders remained undecided until the Peace of Tartu (Dorpat) in 1920. There was also disagreement on Finland's western flanks where the Åland Islands expressed a wish for union with Sweden. Despite a plebiscite in favour of Swedish sovereignty, a League of Nations decision in favour of the broader interests of Finland was accepted and the archipelago became a ninth province of Finland. In Atlantic Scandinavia a plebiscite was held along the German marchlands and a readjustment of Denmark's Jutland border was agreed in favour of the Slesvig Danes. Beyond the seas Iceland acquired a new degree of autonomy in 1918. Meanwhile the collective Scandinavian concern for high-latitude lands brought Norwegian claims for Spitsbergen (Svalbard, in the Old Norse form) which the International High Court at The Hague accepted in 1920. Denmark and Norway brought a dispute over the east coastlands of Greenland before the same body in 1921, when Denmark's sovereignty was affirmed. In the late 1920s, against the background of its growing whaling interests, Norway acquired the Antarctic dependencies of Bouvet and Peter I Islands. Thus the formal delineation of boundaries resolved causes of friction which had disturbed harmony within Scandinavia and were possible causes of complication without.

The foundations of modern Scandinavia were laid in the two generations preceding the First World War, but it is to the two generations succeeding the Versailles Peace that the refinement of so many of Scandinavia's distinguishing features belong. They were not particularly propitious times, but the social upheaval was neither so profound nor so prolonged in Scandinavia as in many countries. The problems that arose were generally modified forms of those that had already troubled other West European nations, but their magnitude was reduced because the number of people affected was smaller and administrators were better equipped to deal with the difficulties. The problems were largely rooted in urbanization. Urban population took precedence over rural population in Denmark and Sweden during the inter-war years; but this situation was delayed in Finland and Iceland until after the Second World War. Simultaneously, industry and manufacturing took the lead from agriculture and raw material production in the economies of the five countries. Both changes assumed greater mobility of people and products. The bicycle that was to become the proverbial means of Danish locomotion and the motor engine that was to release Scandinavian fisherfolk from the vagaries of wind and wave were already widely used by 1914. Automobile, bus and truck only came into their own with improved highway networks, but the technical means for cheap and speedy construction of surfaced highways were unavailable until the 1950s. The modern road system has brought the resources of the entire Scandinavian area into the commercial arena. Engineering developments also helped seagoing, in particular during winter. As a result of the rise of icebreaker fleets in the Baltic, many harbours that were formerly closed in winter are now kept open, while those in the Gulfs of Finland and Bothnia remain open longer. The need for accurate ice forecasting has sharpened another Scandinavian faculty. Once again, the Scandinavians had a fund of experience upon which to build. At an early stage in the development of meteorology, the Norwegian physicist V. Bjerknes pointed the way with a highly original model. Understanding the weather is also crucial for the successful operation of the domestic air services which were to become as intensive in the Scandinavian countries as anywhere in the world.

In the revaluation of resources lay not only the realization of hidden wealth, but also the appreciation that resources were finite. The Scandinavians, with their long experience of resource assessment, were to become increasingly conscious of the need to conserve resources – or at least to maintain them in a state of equilibrium. Representative of their initiative were the national forest surveys conducted in Sweden and Finland in the inter-war years, the first large-scale surveys of their kind in the world. At the international level Norway did much to support the controls of the International Whaling Commission, with its permanent headquarters in Tönsberg, before the decline of the Antarctic hunting grounds.

The conversion of the Scandinavian countries into modern states took place essentially against the background of the economic uncertainties of the inter-war years, the direct military involvement of the 1940s, and the major tasks of material reconstruction during the decade that followed. Although each of the Nordic countries acquired a more distinctive character as a result of these experiences and each emerged more conscious of its vulnerability in an ideologically divided Europe, the outside world began to identify among them a quality which it began to call 'Scandinavian'. For many this quality was inseparable from social and economic policies which anticipated the welfare state. In its externals, the quality was manifested in a new pride of place. Good architects became better when they were given public commissions to embellish the cities of the North with civic buildings – concert halls, museums, galleries, schools. Stockholm town hall was the show piece of the twenties. The fostering of art, expressed in such gestures as the Finnish state pension given to Jean Sibelius and the encouragement given by Oslo city to Gustav Vigeland's park of statuary, became an early practice. In consumer goods as well as in capital goods the object was to equate form and function. Decorative motifs were sought from the past, not least from the Viking Age, and the simple took precedence over the ornate. As a result, by the mid-twentieth century the Scandinavians had become arbiters of modern taste. They appeared equally fertile in proposing solutions to the problems of social organization, so that the voices of their social scientists were heard in the land. A Swedish school of economists sprang out of Knut Wicksell. Edvard Westermarck was a progenitor of contemporary social anthropology; while Gunnar and Alva Myrdal were waiting in the wings to grapple with the social and economic problems of the post-war world. But in attaining the praiseworthy, the Scandinavians automatically exposed themselves to blame. The very word 'Scandinavian', synonym for progressive, was to acquire overtones of licence – if only because (as in the case of Sweden) more enlightened policies towards illegitimacy were initiated and an open approach to family planning had already been adopted in the 1930s. Those who by accident or design attain world leadership, no matter in what sphere, have to endure world criticism.

By the 1930s the Scandinavian countries were becoming increasingly conscious of a sense of political envelopment and increasingly aware that any disruption in Europe would disturb their interrelationships. Partly as a reaction, the foreign ministers of the Nordic countries (including Finland) met annually from 1934 until 1940. In 1935 the Finnish parliament agreed that henceforth it would associate itself with Scandinavian neutrality. Although the common neutral attitudes were more fully formalized two years later, Denmark and Sweden in particular expressed anxiety over defence. Proposals for defensive cooperation, however, made little progress.

After the outbreak of war in 1939 it became clear that the geographical isolation of the Scandinavian countries no longer afforded protection and that the choice of neutrality was not theirs to make. When Russian pressure was exerted directly on Finland in October 1939, the Scandinavian heads of state, together with their foreign ministers, met collectively as a gesture of solidarity. Nevertheless, Russia invaded Finland on 30 November and the resulting Winter War – a part of the legend of Finland – was waged until 12 March 1940. To Finland's heavy losses in men and materials were then added territorial cessions – principal among them south-eastern Karelia with the city of Viipuri – and the problems of resettlement of a refugee population totalling fully 400,000. Within a month of the Russo-Finnish Armistice, Germany, having offered bilateral treaties of non-aggression to all the Scandinavian countries, had invaded Denmark and despatched a fleet to Norway.

Between 1940 and 1944 the 'mighty snake of strife' (as the saga historian Snorri called it) again wormed its way through Scandinavia. With Iceland and the Faeroe Islands occupied by the western powers, Denmark and Norway occupied by Germany, Finland fighting beside (though not allied to) Germany in a Three-Year War (1941–44) against the USSR, Sweden's neutrality made its relations with its Scandinavian neighbours uneasy. It was a neutrality which all would have wished to maintain if they could have done so, but it brought much criticism to Sweden. Two important points need reiteration. Firstly, if it had suited any of the warring powers to implicate Sweden in hostilities rather than to leave it undisturbed, Sweden's declarations of neutrality would have been of little avail. Secondly, the unity of

Scandinavia was better served by Sweden as a neutral than as a belligerent. It was to the good fortune of the Swedes that their country emerged unscathed. It was equally to the good fortune of many neighbouring citizens that Sweden welcomed them during the war years without labour permits, and that when the hostilities were over they had a wealthy friend who was able and willing to give generously for relief and reconstruction in an hour of need.

The armistices in the North did not all come simultaneously. The Russo-Finnish war came to an end in September 1944, following months of deliberations through Stockholm. The hard peace terms called for further territorial cessions – a Soviet military base in Porkkala (to the west of Helsinki, the lease of which was given up in 1955), the Petsamo Corridor, strict restraints on Finnish military forces (which at least relieved Finland of substantial national expenditure), and a heavy reparations programme (to the letter of which Finland complied by August 1952). In 1945, following the collapse of Germany, the occupying troops laid down their arms in Norway and Denmark. Denmark had experienced relatively slight material destruction during the war years; but both Norway (in the counties of Finnmark and Troms) and Finland (in the county of Lappi) had suffered a scorched earth policy at the hands of German forces retreating from the Russians. Rehabilitation of the land – and for Finland resettlement of an eighth of its total population – was to absorb most national energies in the immediate post-war years. Iceland, on the other hand, though resentful of the intrusion upon its sovereignty of British and American troops, nevertheless reaped substantial material benefits from the wartime occupation in the shape of an improved road network. It also became aware of its strategic importance as a north Atlantic air staging post. By the time that hostilities ceased the Scandinavians had realized to the full that they were an integral part of Europe and that their corporate unity was inseparable from the unity of Europe.

Since 1945 the five countries have sharpened their individual personalities and strengthened the sympathetic bonds that bind them together. They have witnessed the fulfilment of many desires and the realization of many devices that they have long coveted. Moreover, because for so much of the last century and a half they have appeared as relatively poor neighbours in Europe, they have not suffered the myth that the last century was a golden age. In general, they feel no sense of regression, because it is only during the last generation that they have escaped from the problems of economic and social transition into modern states. In so doing, they have entered an age of transmission, giving more than they receive; for, in learning the arts of fuller living, they have acquired the means of more generous giving. Although their modest size suggests that they are likely to continue more influenced than influencing in world affairs, their impact grows out of all proportion to the numbers of their inhabitants.

1

2

3

4

5

6

7

8

Scandinavian faces.
1 Tollund man, a Dane of 2,000 years ago.
2 Dane of today.
3 Icelandic fisherman.
4 Swedish farmer.
5 Norwegian athlete.
6 Finn from North Karelia. 7 Lapp wearing a 'Four Wind' cap. 8 Greenland woman enjoying a cigar.

9 Surtsey, Iceland's
youngest volcano, which
began to erupt from the
sea in 1963, and has now
formed an island.

10 Steam springs, another
volcanic feature of the
Icelandic scene.

11 In Sweden's Jämtland, distant mountains and rivers nourish an important hydro-electric system, and forests supply the wood-working industry.

12 Åland, the mid-Baltic province of Finland, consists of more than six thousand islands, only eighty of them inhabited. The islands, red-rocked and pine-clad, are typical of the Baltic archipelagos.

13 *Opposite:* Sheer mountainous rocks tower above the fishing community of Svolvær, in the Lofoten Islands, North Norway.

14 The landscape around Langaa in Jutland – flat country on the margin of the West Danish heathlands.

15 Snow may be one of Scandinavia's chief enemies, but it provides ample opportunities for the skiers of Norway, Sweden and Finland. Even city-dwellers are rarely far from ski tracks, and these citizens of Oslo are within easy reach of the centre of the capital. In summer the equally accessible Oslofjord offers them the delights of sailing and swimming.

16 In the Baltic, ice is a major problem and the fleet of icebreakers is kept busy from late November until late May. Generally channels for shipping can be kept clear, but about once every decade there is a winter so hard that the icebreakers themselves are defeated, and must wait for some clearance of the pack ice which gathers around them.

17 With spring comes the release of Walpurgis Night (30 April), and Helsinki students, in their white caps, make merry with balloons and unmusical instruments.

Part Two   The Scandinavian countries

4   Everyday life

THE SCANDINAVIANS of today are engaged in a perpetual if gentle tug-of-war between the assertion of their identities as individual countries, and the maintenance of a common pattern of daily life. It is a pattern which derives from their racial relationship, from climate and latitude, and from a common background of social and economic history. These factors combined dominate the purely geographical setting, itself more likely to divide than to unite. The fisher farmer of Norway's fjords must order his life in a different way from the forest farmer of northern Sweden and Finland, or the farmer, pure and simple, of the neatly manicured plains of Denmark.

Yet the similarities between the daily rounds of Scandinavia are strong. They often absorb and always dwarf the differences. They provoke the further comparison and contrast between the Baltic and the Mediterranean, the two poles, the point and counterpoint of Western Europe. Here are two great inland seas, patterned with islands, almost tideless yet demanding considerable gifts of navigation, and each surrounded by peoples who have often warred against each other, yet retained a fundamental relationship. But in the context of Europe, the Baltic and the Mediterranean have fostered ways of life totally and absolutely different. In the Mediterranean, the basis of daily life is compounded of sun, grape and olive; in the Baltic, ice, potato (either the dreary boiled accompaniment of too many meals, or, when converted, the too potent schnapps) and the salted herring which brings to the tongue that sharpness of flavour that the olive has done since time immemorial.

Today, artificial heat, modern machinery, canned and frozen foods and the like have come to the North, but dented only slightly the old traditions. The social centre of the Mediterranean world is the market place or the café; of the North, the home. Mediterranean man is historically a city-dweller; Northern man is a countryman who would often prefer to shun his cities because they stand between him and his smaller ration of warmth and sun. Mediterranean man has talked and philosophized in the open air. Northern man has battled with a climate which demands action and activity and leaves little time or energy for abstract theorizing. The strangest of the contrasts between North and South lies in their politico-social framework. The democracy seeded in the Mediterranean has there given place to more autocratic régimes and aristocratic societies; in the North it has rooted itself more firmly, perhaps, than anywhere else in Europe, and given to daily life a greater relaxation than is often found elsewhere.

Within the North itself, life has its sharp, dramatic polarities. For long months of winter, much of Scandinavia lies in the grip of ice, snow, and darkness. And then comes the brief summer, dazzling and brilliant, when the sun has barely time to set before it must rise again. Ice and snow, above all else, form the background against which most of the Scandinavians must adapt their daily lives. Winter is the real constant of existence, capable of mitigation but not of fundamental change. Modern technology can reduce its power but never defeat it. In the North, it remains a dictator, inflicting, according to latitude, frozen seas and lakes, an unending snow cover, or, worst of all, greyness and slush. Houses and blocks of flats demand (but do not invariably receive) impeccable construction, deep foundations and thermal installations well protected from frost. Double windows and double doors are taken for granted, and in many public buildings doors can be pushed open only with a strength of arm not possessed by all. Many of the architects of post-war Scandinavia have shown a brilliant inventiveness which has made it possible to build in a way which repels the weather but pleases the eye. An earlier generation of architects made an almost brutal transition from the picturesque old wooden buildings of the nineteenth century to heavy, near-pompous weather-defiant edifices. Yet wood – and wooden houses still remain here and there in the country – is an unexpectedly warm building material, and the decorative ceiling-high porcelain stoves of the North can be tamed into giving out a heat almost as even as modern central heating. In fact, it is still easier to feel cold indoors in some more temperate parts of Europe than it is anywhere in the North.

And it is far, far easier for life to be disrupted by a mild snowfall. In Scandinavia (as in much of North America) snow is a costly item. In Finland, for instance, the cost of winter, in its broadest sense, is reckoned the equivalent of a quarter of the State budget, but it poses few problems which cannot be overcome. The snow ploughs come out, the tram and railway lines are kept clear, air services continue as usual, and the citizens themselves sweep snowless the stretch of pavement outside their own homes. Motorists equip their cars with winter tyres; and if they do skid on the treacherous layer of ice that forms on top of frozen snow, they can set themselves to rights with extraordinary speed. Sometimes, indeed, communications may be easier. Horses with jingling bells and sleigh belong now to the romantic past, but in the countryside skis will carry their wearers across fields and frozen lakes which could not be traversed in summer. Sometimes, in fact, 'as the crow flies' is almost the equivalent of 'as the skis glide'. The chilliest of winter pastimes continue. The avid fisherman will not allow a layer of ice to stand between him and the object of his passions, and ice-hole fishing is a regular winter sport. Likewise thousands of well-upholstered city-dwellers, many of them members of a form of 'ice-hole club', jump daily into holes in the ice specially prepared for them. But the occasional desperately hard winter can bring havoc, as in 1966, when the icebreakers themselves were trapped in the Baltic; or as in 1940 when, in the Winter War, Russian forces were able to encircle and defeat the doughty Finns by bringing their tanks across the frozen Gulf of Finland.

Even in less fearsome years the difference between outdoor and indoor temperatures has a high nuisance value, in terms of clothing. Indoors efficient heating and tightly closed windows can easily bring the temperature up to an airless 75°F; outdoors it may be below zero, plus a biting wind which makes it feel at least twenty-five below. Such variations need several layers of clothing, and a lengthy discarding, indoors, of heavy topcoats, fur hats, thick stockings, high boots and, in the slush of the towns, that dreariest of all footwear – galoshes. All this makes a fortune for the individuals in charge of cloakrooms in restaurants who expect tips in the grand manner; but, one wonders, how much trade do department stores lose when fur-clad women (and even fur-clad men) escape from their stifling heat rather than complete their shopping?

Winter gives a certain grim earnestness to daily life in the North but it does not interfere with its general enjoyment. Indeed, it is the season when social life reaches a climax. There are parties, concerts, theatres, operas as elsewhere. There are also, for the Norwegians, the Swedes and the Finns, winter sports on the doorstep and special ski-ing holidays for the schools around the end of February, when there is plenty of snow and the sun begins to gather strength. The worst side of the winter for the Scandinavians is rain and greyness. This can almost be guaranteed anywhere in November and part of December; it can continue through the winter in Denmark, punctuated by inter-mittent light snow and always accompanied by wind. The Atlantic coast winter is more often than not chill and damp; farther east it can be much colder but dry and invigorating. But everywhere in the North there develops, about March, the malady known as 'spring tiredness'; a malady not unknown elsewhere, but accentuated there by the length of the winter, the shortness of the days, and the long wait for the real rushing and riotous spring which comes after the months known as 'spring winter' to differentiate them from 'high winter'.

Spring in the North, however dramatic, can be very short and the Scandinavians think of it more as the herald of summer than as a season in its own right. For them, the line would run: 'If spring comes, can summer be far behind?' And with the summer, an almost total change in the pattern of daily life. If the business of earning a living did not have to continue, one suspects that the majority of Scandi-navians would slip for three months into a trance-like beatitude induced by sun and water, forest and solitude. As it is, the working world half-bows to the sun and allows shorter hours, longer week-ends. There are various ways of shortening working time in the summer, but the most admirable seems to be the Norwegian abolition of the afternoon. All the year round, work starts at eight and goes on until three, with only a break of twenty minutes or so for coffee and sandwiches brought from home. Then, after three, there is still time and light in winter for ski-ing, except in the far north. In summer some offices shut at two – and that leaves eight or nine hours of sun-light for sailing, swimming and other outdoor sports. These hours are precious to sportsmen and women as zestful as the Scandinavians, for whom personal activity means far, far more than spectator sports.

The centre of life shifts away from the towns and to the countryside, lakeshore or seashore. Ownership of 'a little place in the country', be it no more than a primitive shack or an entire island in one of the Baltic archipelagos, is the norm for dustman or diplomat. The dustman has probably built his own one-room shack on cheaper and less sought-after land away from any stretch of water; but the diplomat asks only the extra comfort that is provided by rather more space. Life must be simplified, work reduced to a minimum so that summer can be above all a time of freedom and liberation. A site near water is most coveted because the Scandinavians are amphibious creatures for whom, until recently, a yacht or a motor boat was a possession more highly regarded than an automobile. For them all it provides the sport they enjoy the most, apart from ski-ing; and for many it is the only form of transport between their island summer cottage and the nearest general stores. A few unfortunate folk are still dependent on a rowing boat to cover shorter distances, and the old Finnish proverb 'The man steers, the woman rows' still retains an element of truth.

Scandinavia was a two-house society long before the possession of a holiday cottage or flat had become a status symbol farther west. On the other hand, it regards holiday hotels as the preserve of foreign tourists, who are pitied, rather than envied, by those who can relax in the solitude of their own surroundings. (Although they have made the Canary Islands and Majorca, in winter, seem almost like tropical complements of Scandinavia.) But in Scandinavia the idyllic has passed its peak. Better roads, better public transport and more cars mean that more people can make greater use of holiday houses. Some have been modernized by bottled gas and 'winterized' by central heating and double-glazing so that they can be used at the weekend all the year round. Now there are long stretches of waterfront where private ownership prevents access by the general public, and legislation has come too late to save precious areas of sea- and lake-shore for the people as a whole. A humbler alternative to a second home, eagerly sought and tended by city-dwellers, is a plot in one of the many 'colony gardens' outside the towns. This is an allotment on a generous scale where flowers, fruit and vegetables can be grown, and where there is still space for the handy Northerner to build a one-room hut; not large, but better than a tent and as good as many caravans for weekend habitation.

The hunger for sun and air has led naturally to a large allowance of paid holidays for both industrial and office workers. No one in Scandinavia has less than three weeks a year, and many have four.

Schools have three months' holiday in summer, so it is not unusual for mothers and children to spend the whole period in the country, while husbands commute as best they can, either daily or only at weekends. Work continues through the summer, but *pianissimo*, and the chances of completing any sizeable transactions between mid-summer day and the end of August are fairly slender.

Indeed, an Anglo-Saxon arriving in Scandinavia with business intent around midsummer would have as much chance of immediate progress as would a Martian arriving in Britain on Christmas Eve. Midsummer is the festival second only to Christmas in the Scandinavian year, and there are some who hold it even more important. Both, as primarily pagan celebrations, are associated with the cult of the tree which goes far back in Northern mythology, and particularly with the forbidding 'world tree', which connected heaven, earth and hell and all living creatures. The 'world tree' was thought to be the ash, but its derivatives of today are the Christmas tree, the maypole, and the birch. The maypole has no connection with the month of May, having found its name in the Old Norse verb *maja*, to adorn. All over Scandinavia it is the symbol of midsummer, though in the Åland Islands it stands elaborately adorned all the summer through and sometimes all the year round. The birch is the more personal midsummer symbol, the tree for which the Scandinavians have their own special attachment. In its various species it is said to possess magical and luck-bearing properties, while the leafy branches of the rarer scented birch (*Betula odorata*) are considered indispensable in Finland to the ritual of the sauna, leaving their fragrance on the perspiring skin which they have gently beaten. Great branches or, near the high fells, bundles of dwarf birch are brought into the houses at midsummer. They are also used to decorate cars, and before the advent of the more streamlined diesel locomotives, were sometimes incongruously entwined round the ancient railway engines which chugged their way on wood-power.

Midsummer celebrations often begin with the sauna, the Finnish 'bath', which has now spread, in adequate reproductions and spurious imitations, far beyond Finland. Then there are the bonfires, lit for Saint John the Baptist, as they are still in some parts of France. They flame the most splendidly on the seashore, the islands, or the promontories reaching out into the lakes. Then it seems almost as if the fires are holding a dialogue among themselves, and those who have built them feel a sense of community with the more distant fire-tenders. And, of course, there is outdoor dancing and merrymaking on this, the briefest (and most alcoholic) night of the year. For this is the almost spontaneous celebration of the most joyous moment of the Northern climatic year; Christmas, instead, is a defensive prophylaxis against what might otherwise be its most despairing days.

So against the all-pervasive gloom of November and December is set a round of sometimes slightly artificial gaiety which puts a heavy strain on most of the population. Offices, clubs and all kinds of organizations and cohesive groups have, at some time in December, their own 'Little Christmas' – an informal party well laced with food and drink, song and dance. On 13 December (the shortest day of the year by the old calendar) Swedish-speaking Scandinavia celebrates the festival of Saint Lucia, whose name has made her the patroness of light. At home, the celebrations are simple. A daughter in her teens, dressed in white and wearing a crown dangerously mounted with lighted candles, takes coffee to the rest of the family before they get up. In schools, offices and factories, other candle-lit blondes assume the role of Lucia. And in towns the saint has become a beauty queen, chosen by ballot, who rides through the streets to functions in aid of charities.

Meanwhile the housewife's burden grows daily heavier. In Christmas-tree country a fir-tree in the house is almost mandatory; so are a wealth of decorations and a multiplicity of candles of all shapes and colours – the last a common year-round feature of Scandinavian homes. Baking occupies days and days in December; and then for Christmas Eve the mammoth Christmas ham must be prepared. For in the North the traditions of Christmas are the traditions of the countryside; pork represents the pig that was killed before Christmas, to provide, as well as the Christmas Eve feast, the sausages and ham that would keep for several months. Neither turkey nor goose has ever been associated with Northern Christmas. The pork is generally excellent and admirably cooked; but the same cannot be said of the two other traditional dishes: a particularly pungent variety of lime-cured dried fish, and a rice pudding so plain that most of the rest of Europe would have refused it in the nursery. One has to remind oneself that not so many decades ago, rice was an imported delicacy, exotic and costly.

Christmas, as everywhere, is a family celebration; but in the Northern countries there are probably more purely personal festivities than elsewhere because the opportunities for public entertainment, though growing fast now, have never been very great. Confirmation, a ceremony which shows no signs of decline despite dwindling church membership, entails family parties and a round of often elaborate gifts. When a boy or girl passes the 'student examination', the last exam of the school career, allowing entrance to the university, the celebration thereof, with its formal clothes, student caps and bouquets of red roses, surpasses anything comparable elsewhere. So do the observations of the fiftieth and all succeeding decennial birthdays. (An insatiable curiosity about other people's ages is an inexplicable Scandinavian characteristic.) Some people obviously enjoy these junketings, which may begin as early as 7.30 a.m. with friends making the obligatory well-wishing call on their way to work. But there is a growing tendency to take flight, the victims quite rightly observing that a few days in an expensive hotel abroad costs no more than the food and drink they would be obliged to provide for all their guests, whom custom allows to come without invitation.

The scale of these festivities is all the more surprising in view of the small size of the average Scandinavian home and the fact that the average wife goes out to a job, and has no help in the house. There is a good deal of the paradox in the whole Nordic attitude to living space. As long as a quarter of a century ago Scandinavians could be heard to observe that their womenfolk would never put up with the standards of building and equipment accepted in much of Europe. And, indeed, the fitted kitchen and many other improvements in dwellings of today have come largely from Scandinavia. But the Scandinavians rarely seem to have grasped that most of Europe would never put up with the really cramped quarters in which the North continues to live today. Of course, there are good-sized houses and good-sized flats to be had, particularly among those built earlier in the century; and the trend today is towards a modest increase in space. But it is not unusual to find a family of four living in two or three rooms. The bedroom used only for sleeping in is often regarded as a plain waste of good space, and a divan in the living-room is luxurious if compared with the shake-down in the kitchen, which is considered a perfectly adequate sleeping area, and one that can be offered to guests without shame or excuse.

Against this lack of elbow room can be set the fact that slums are almost unknown in the Northern countries. But it is not altogether easy to explain why the Scandinavians, with their love of home and their traditions of hospitality, should have continued to hem themselves in as they have. As can be seen in the old houses moved from the countryside to the outdoor Folk Museums which are a special feature of the Scandinavian countries, it was a traditional custom to live, eat and sleep in the same room. So, presumably, it was accepted when large blocks of modern flats came to be built in the cities. Finland, Norway and Sweden, with their low population density, could in theory have allowed their towns to spread out farther – as, in fact, some of the new towns are doing, although another school of town-planners is opting for compactness and rejecting areas of green as 'waste space'. And today building costs are often a deciding factor. Foundations which reach below the frost line have often to be quarried through granite; and although the Scandinavians have developed remarkable techniques of building during hard winter weather, it remains a far more difficult operation than in milder climes.

Fortunately, most Northerners are neat and orderly, well organized and practical in the arrangement of their possessions. This sense of order, often design, extends to their food. Even the smallholder's wife in the Arctic wilderness has the knack of forming her bread into pleasing shapes, and in almost any home food is arranged and 'trimmed' to make it attractive to the eye as well as to the palate. Until a few years ago, the Scandinavians themselves would not have claimed much of a place in the league tables of the international cuisine. Only their 'cold table', composed principally of their many excellent native fish, both fresh and cured, and cold meats, gave them any sort of reputation abroad. More recently canned and frozen fruit and vegetables and imported foods have made Scandinavian meals, especially in restaurants and hotels, more comparable with what one might find elsewhere in the northern half of Europe, providing one excepts on the one hand, slowness of service, and on the other, the more exotic and occasional baby bear, reindeer meat and lampreys. One must also except the spectacle – unseen outside the more expensive restaurants of Sweden and Finland – of a diner of middle age or more, half hidden behind an outsize and colourful plastic bib, gorging himself on crayfish and schnapps. The season – roughly August and part of September – when small crayfish are netted from the Northern fresh waters, also provides the pretext for innumerable parties in the home, where the inexorable rule of one glass of schnapps to every crayfish eaten promotes hilarity in record time. But even the most fastidious cannot eat crayfish without getting liberally dowsed by the water their small forms retain, and plastic provides both protection and comedy.

Drink, unfortunately, is not often a source of comedy in Scandinavia. The local schnapps comes in varying qualities, ranging from something resembling firewater to a more refined spirit. But crude or refined, the Northerners find it difficult to drink it in moderation, and an entire bottle can be emptied at a phenomenal speed. The Scandinavians rightly point out that, man for man, year for year, their total consumption of alcohol is less than that of several other countries, including the United States, France and Germany. But one would probably be right in assuming that in Scandinavia consumption is concentrated into far shorter periods of time than elsewhere, and that plain drunkenness, as opposed to mildly chronic alcoholism, is more common than elsewhere. One can point to many reasons: the cold and the long darkness of winter, the potency of the native product, and the fact that there are few bars or cafés – except in Denmark – where people can drop in for only a couple of quick drinks instead of having the whole bottle at their elbow at home.

Governments have in their different ways wrestled with the problem for decades and have up to a point contained it, though no more. For many years Sweden had an elaborate rationing system which had a small measure of success but seemed to concentrate the mind of the population more firmly than ever on the subject. Rationing was eventually abandoned in the fifties, and while consumption increased, it did not do so on a spectacular scale. The Finns still have a vague rationing system, and almost everywhere there are other deterrents. In Finland, Norway and Sweden the sale of liquor is the monopoly of the state, which has its own shops. They are fairly accessible in the big towns, but people living in small places and in the country may have to travel as much as fifty miles to acquire a bottle. There are still many hotels which may not sell spirits, though more can sell wines. The Finns have done well with their scheme of punishment for drivers found in charge of cars with only a minute quantity of alcohol in their systems. A few months of heavy manual work, often road-making, is the penalty meted out to all and sundry, whether cabinet ministers or workmen more used to such tasks. The Norwegians have subsidized boys' brass bands out of funds earmarked for temperance propaganda, with the infallible reasoning that one cannot blow and drink at the same time. In the long run more will probably be achieved by the encouragement, tax-wise, of table wines, and by the growth of the slightly more sophisticated social climate in which such wines are favoured at the expense of more potent spirits. In the meantime, illicit distilling and smuggling remain widespread.

The Scandinavians tend towards addiction to two other liquids, coffee and milk. The coffee kettle, in which grounds are boiled and reboiled, resides permanently on hob or stove, and can – sometimes must – be offered to all comers at all times of day. Milk, except in Denmark, is drunk instead of water at most meals in the home and many in restaurants. It is also consumed in large quantities in other forms, as buttermilk, or the local variety of yoghourt. This is only one small aspect of the whole agricultural-economic problem of Scandinavia, where dairy products have run into surplus. However, the North still manages to absorb large quantities of home-produced milk and cheese. Food in the home generally remains rather plain, with potatoes and salt fish as constant reminders of the days when poverty enforced a self-sufficient but extremely limited diet, in winter especially. Another reminder is the ritual autumn search in the woods and fields for edible fungi and wild berries to break the gastronomic monotony.

In the home, mealtimes can be elastic, not to say erratic. In families with children it is fairly common to have dinner at 5.30 or 6, by which time workers and schoolchildren have all come home. But later hours are gradually becoming more usual, particularly when guests are entertained. And in Sweden especially, there are formalities which must be observed. The host, having escorted the principal lady guest to the table, makes a short speech of welcome at the beginning of the meal. The principal male guest makes a speech of thanks at the end, before the guests leave the table. The host, with the principal lady on his arm, is the last to leave the dining-room, in order, it is frivolously observed, to make sure that none of the table silver has been pocketed by the guests.

But on the whole, formality is not a characteristic of the day-to-day life of the North. Class distinctions have never been strongly marked, and the tendency of the times is to make them progressively less so. Socially, individuals do not feel themselves markedly superior or inferior to each other, although some of their customs have a touch of the hierarchical. The individual must, as far as possible, be identified for what he is. If he has a university degree, either 'Doctor' or 'Master' will always precede his name, particularly in writing. This is a fairly simple matter, and possibly stems from the great respect for education inculcated by the Lutheran Church. But things become far more complicated when people have to be identified by their position in their firm, and addressed as 'Office Manager Anderson' or 'Director's Assistant Carlson'. Moreover, Mr Anderson or Mr Carlson may be mortally offended if they are assigned a lower place than they hold in the hierarchy, or if their promotion has been overlooked. And even Mr Anderson's nine-year-old son is used to seeing his letters addressed to 'Schoolboy Johannes Anderson'.

However, these are local quirks, rather than deeply-rooted characteristics. Day-to-day social life throughout the North is above all easy and democratic. Relations are generally unstrained, whether between governors and governed, employers and employed, well-to-do and not so well-to-do. The Scandinavians have never been much afflicted by false respect for their 'betters'. In countries with small populations too many people are known personally to each other for pretence or pretentiousness to gain a real hold.

5   Denmark

DENMARK (*Danmark* to the Danes) is the smallest of the Scandinavian states, the most fragmented, the most favourably situated, the most densely peopled and the most vulnerable to outside pressures. In the east, for all practical purposes, it is integrated across the Sound with Sweden. To the south, its island promontories point to those of north Germany, while a Versailles boundary divides West Germany from Denmark through the neck of Jutland. It is 400 miles over the North Sea (*Vesterhavet* to the Danes) to eastern England. Denmark, which enjoys the least inclement of Scandinavia's climes, is also distinctive in Scandinavia because of the high proportion of its cultivated and occupied area. Although ten per cent of its area remains under wood-land, it is tamed and disciplined woodland. The eight per cent still under heath, bog and dune may appear to be intractable, though it would not be beyond the capacity of the Danes to transform it. But Denmark, the most metropolitan of the Scandinavian lands and with the greatest pressure on living space, has come to regard the conservation of its residual natural areas as an important object in national policy.

The stork's-eye view of Denmark is first of an exposed coast with sweeping bights where the shingle skips upon the longest sand beaches in Europe as it is pounded by a North Sea more grey than blue. Behind them the strong west winds have built up a cordillera of dunes which, from the Skaw in the north to Blaavands Huk in the south, is scarcely broken. Extensive lagoons such as that of Ringkøbing have developed where the westward-flowing streams have been ponded back. South of the Huk, the dunes have been breached in historic times. As along the coast of Germany and the Netherlands, the shallow Wadden Sea that has resulted from the invasion has tidal mudflats and saltmarshes. The channels that led through them to medieval ports, such as Ribe, have been silted up. The grassy dikes of the empoldered lands gradually win back the lost territory.

The dunes, restless and untamed, have regularly encroached upon the Jutish farmlands. Marram grass, wiry and rhizome-rooted, partly fixes them: plantations of pines, drawn up like military battalions, strive to contain them. The dunes have a seasonal attraction in their own right, as summer cabins attest; but the holiday atmosphere along the coast of Vesterhavet is unsophisticated and robust. The starve-all heaths to the east – cut over, burnt over, trampled over, grazed over and generally sapped of their substance since prehistoric times – have been slowly nursed back to health. Marl, humus, stable manure, artificial fertilizer, rotation cropping, draining and hedging have improved soil structure and water balance. Peatlands have been reclaimed, too; though meres and ponds, relics of peat diggings, remain. The streams – once slippery with eels – that thread their way across the gentle, often imperceptible, slopes of west Jutland, have been trapped and tapped to serve the water meadows. The lines that men have drawn upon the face of west Jutland are much straighter than those in other parts of Denmark. Their regularity, favoured by flat land, recalls the para-military occupation of the empty heaths two centuries ago and the near mathematical planning of farmsteads, supply centres and amenities.

By contrast, east Jutland is hilly, its modest summits are pimpled with tumuli; their intervening hollows are dimpled with lakes. Settlement is concentrated in nucleated villages and substantial towns which are linked by a highly irregular network of communications. The hill country, furrowed by valleys steep-sided as railway cuttings and bearing beechwoods, is intruded upon by the deep inlets of the Kattegat. At the head of these inlets are old-established seaports. From south to north, formerly Danish Flensborg is succeeded by Aabenraa, Kolding, Fredericia (the bridgetown of the Little Belt), Vejle, Horsens, Jutland's capital of Aarhus, Mariager and Limfjord's twin city of Aalborg-Nørresundby. Limfjord's battery of cement plants marks the limits of large-scale industry, though remoter Vendsyssel supports ferry ports and fishing harbours such as Fredrikshavn and Hirtshals. The mood of Vendsyssel is a compound of the perceptive myths of Johannes V. Jensen, of the realism of the late nineteenth-century artists' colony of Skagen, and of the opportunism of those who encourage a lively tourist trade. Beyond the successive lighthouses that identify the Skaw, where Jutland dissolves into treacherous waters as a submarine spit, visitors may stand right foot in the Baltic and left foot in the North Sea and survey the line of masts that symbolize the tragedies of countless ships that the centuries have cast upon the sands.

Archipelago Denmark, though not without the sterility and isolation of the remoter parts of Jutland, contains the climax of Denmark's fruitfulness, productivity and wealth. Sjælland, the largest island, has the greatest concentration of population, industry and commerce. The development of Ørestad, the name for the megapolis that is emerging about the Sound, is likely to exaggerate the disparity of wealth and opportunity in the different parts of Denmark. An integrated complex of four million inhabitants is expected to have developed there by about the year 2000. Around the core of a genial countryside there are other towns which benefit from the nearby presence of this complex – Korsør on the Great Belt ferry route, Kalundborg, point of departure to Jutland, Næstved and Vordingborg (with Denmark's longest bridge). The communicational axis that links Sjælland and Jutland also brings prosperity to the centrally situated island of Fyn, popularly called the 'garden of Denmark'. Odense, its comfortable city port and university town, is complemented by south-coast idylls such as Faaborg. South of Fyn and Sjælland the archipelago is more fragmented, though its divided waters often look more like lakes than the sea. To the east, there is the flash of pinnacled chalk cliffs in the island of Møn. Complementary to this central cluster of islands are others scattered in near-radial distraction. The pancake flats of sandy Læsø and sandier Anholt make unexpected appearances in the Kattegat; rocky Bornholm, in the south central Baltic, suffers the extremity of detachment.

The stork's-eye view (and even more the view from an aircraft) conceals as much as it reveals. It recognizes a land of relatively diverse character, although the diversity is declared in a low key. It observes the stamp of homogeneity placed upon it by an industrious people and the signs of a rougher natural world that they have left around its edges. But the view is oversimplified. At the same time, the outer world imagines Denmark to be a Hans Christian Andersen country, painted in bold primary colours. In some respects this is a false image. In other respects, the Denmark of today is more bold and colourful than in Hans Andersen's day. The highly organized contemporary scene is partly a product of Europe's industrial revolution and partly the result of Denmark's development as an industrial country in its own right. In Andersen's Denmark, as in Charles Dickens's England, there was much poverty and pain. Within living memory, as is shown by the daguerreotypes and photographs of the day, the underdeveloped country of Denmark suffered much rural depression. Although the influence of revolutionary France brought about sufficient rural and political reform for it to be claimed that the old order was buried beneath the dynastic monuments in Roskilde Cathedral, dissatisfaction lingered. For all the illumination promised to rural society when the first Folk High School at Rødding came into being in south Jutland in 1844, and for all the improvements consequent upon the development of co-operative marketing and purchase, it is a significant reflection of Danish attitudes that the radical philosophy of Henry George should have carried so much weight before the First World War. And while, by comparison with those of later nineteenth-century London or Paris, the streets of Copenhagen could scarcely have had twilight areas, they elicited novels of protest from such authors as Holger Drachmann. On the plinth of the memorial to King Frederik VII which stands in front of Christiansborg is inscribed the motto 'the strength of kings reposes in the happiness of their peoples'. The material bases of potential happiness had still to await the passage of several decades before the strength could be assured. The manicured well-served countryside and the cosy well-kept towns, seen from the windows of faintly old-fashioned railway carriages or over the handlebars of the still ubiquitous bicycle, are the product of the twentieth century.

The forward thrust of farming awaited co-operative organization and mechanization. Mechanization has changed Danish farming operations in two ways. In stage one it revolutionized the processing of farm products, subsequently helping to rationalize operations on the small holdings by scaling down equipment – milking machines, tractors, harvesting equipment – to meet their purses. In the second and contemporary stage the shadow of the factory farm hangs over the industry. The mixed holding, focusing upon owner-operator, milk cow and bacon pig, and dependent upon a web of co-operative organization, suffers an increasingly narrow profit margin. Farm amalgamation and battery production are inevitable developments. In contrast to other Scandinavian countries, Denmark has no problem of farm abandonment, although it is asserted that in recent years an average of twenty farms a day have been ceasing to operate on independent lines. Each year thousands of its farming fraternity are finding their way into workshops, factories and services.

In a way, Danish agriculture is suffering from its very success. Surplus production, the result of the widespread adoption of scientific farming practices, is an embarrassment. While the miracle of Danish farming is a model for the world, demand for its products has not increased as swiftly as supply – this despite superior quality and expert salesmanship. It is barely a generation since Danes were eating margarine in order to release butter for export. The market for dairy produce is now depressed not only by price, but also by the association of butter, cream and animal fats with coronary heart disease. Farmers have a certain room for manoeuvre. For example, beef production (recalling the medieval export of cattle on the hoof) is a partial substitute for dairying. However, beef farming is in general less well suited to the structure of the Danish farm. Again, although industry can extend the range of products based on the farmer's raw materials, manufacturing ingenuity has its bounds. There is a limit to the amount of barley needed by brewers; potatoes, by distillers; sugar beet, by confectioners; hogs, by pork processors. To visit any of the dozens of agricultural shows that occupy the summer calendar – above all the Bellahøj fair outside Copenhagen – is to bask in the sun of the farmers' achievements.

One rural feature that distinguishes Denmark from the rest of Scandinavia is the extent of horticulture. Horticulture is historically associated with the Dutch settlement of Copenhagen's suburban island of Amager; and there remains an almost Netherlandish concern with fruit, vegetables and flowers. Today Denmark supports more than 10,000 horticultural establishments. The glow of Danish apples and the even deeper glow imparted by morello cherries to brandy are Danish features long established in the Scandinavian market. Virtually every farm has its modest orchard and burgeoning garden, while most townsfolk are as green-fingered as their country cousins. The per capita purchase of cut flowers, admittedly cheaper in Denmark, is higher than anywhere else in flower-conscious Scandinavia; while acres of greenhouses provide the *exotica* that are an integral feature of home and public building alike. It goes without saying that a people so fastidious about its private use of flowers should demand their generous employment in public places. The royal castles, above all Frederiksborg, retain their eighteenth-century gardens. Railway stations and quaysides display their rose beds; while roadsides and railway embankments have a happy habit of breaking into naturalized stretches of lilac and *Rosa rugosa*.

The stresses of farming are partly redressed by the successes of industry, for according to statistics of employment and of output by value, Denmark is essentially a manufacturing country. In contrast to the limited range of farm produce, there is growing diversity in almost every field of manufacturing. The techno-chemical industry has its florescence of enzymes and albumens; the pharmaceutical industry, its infinity of medicaments. It is a far cry from the simple cream separator to the continuous butter-making machine; from crude concrete to fast-coloured, petrifying, water-repellent cement coatings; from craft-based cabinet-making to the continually renewing designs of Denmark's world-renowned furniture industry; from the shipwrights who build the west coast's wooden fishing boats to those in the east-coast yards that construct specialized shipping for the markets of the world.

At the same time, there is more room for flexibility of unit size in the industrial than in the agricultural arena. By European standards, Denmark is not a country of large-scale industrial enterprise. The Carlsberg-Tuborg merger and the engineering company of Danfoss, both employing a labour force of about 8,000, are exceptional in size. Half Denmark's industrial establishments have less than a hundred employees. If small size restricts research and retraining, it is partly compensated by the facilities for them provided by trade associations. Shop-floor relations are certainly more relaxed in small concerns. Industry, located principally in towns and cities, moves increasingly to green field locations around their edges. An interesting adjustment to size is the provision of collective industrial factories where a number of smaller concerns can operate under one roof.

Danish industry has a long experience of raw material deficiencies. Old-established industries, such as those based upon native hardwoods, have come to rely increasingly on imported timber. Tropical hardwoods on the one hand and softwood products on the other are imports indispensable to a diversity of manufactures. Some industries, such as those based on copra and oil seeds, have relied upon imported raw materials from the beginning. The modern machine and shipbuilding industries look to specialist steels imported from all over the Continent. As a land without significant supplies of indigenous fuel, Denmark depends upon overseas supplies. Britain, Germany and Poland competed for its coal trade in pre-war days. Since oil replaced coal, Denmark has benefited from several large-scale refineries which yield a wide range of petro-chemical byproducts. Prospectively, North Sea gas from Danish fields should reduce the high fuel bill. The streamlined yet complex refineries are the antitheses of the work-shops and studios that yield the silverware of Georg Jensen, the shadowy blues and dove greys of Royal Copenhagen porcelain, the buffs and moccas of supple suede and leatherware, the honey-coloured beads of polished amber. It is inevitable that new factories should intrude upon the landscape. The response is to make them architec-tural features of interest in their own right. Occasionally, they display inspired gestures, such as the Angli shirt factory at Herning, with its immense courtyard ceramic.

As in all the Scandinavian countries, industry is unevenly distri-buted. There are no seriously underprivileged areas in Denmark, but there are 'grey' areas. The outlying islands suffer differential popula-tion migration and have little attractive power for industry. The rate of economic development of north Jutland is also slower than that for most of the country. These peripheral areas may look prosperous enough to the casual visitor; but they are upon the threshold of stagnation and are territories of concern for Denmark's regional planners. They are also areas which qualify for financial support.

The expansion of industry is accompanied by intensified urbaniza-tion. As the smallest of the Scandinavian countries with the least amount of spare land, Danes are very conscious of the way that the town is trespassing upon the countryside. It is estimated that the current rate of consumption of land by bricks and mortar is two square kilometres a week. Admittedly, it is intelligently used space – where planners have elaborated pedestrian precincts, accommodated the continuingly ubiquitous bicycle, remembered the popular colony gardens, made provision for the sick and the old, created adventure playgrounds and 'youth towns', and even conceived designs for communal living. Trespass upon farmland may matter less when there is a surplus of farm products and when there is a measure of adjustment through the reclamation of coastal areas. But the threat is not directed entirely against farmland. Competition for land use is inevitably a challenge to Denmark's well-established conservation districts and protected areas of outstanding natural beauty. It is estimated, for example, that the 100,000 summer villas (privately and institutionally owned) will be multiplied fivefold in the next decade. There is also recurrent concern for the position of ancient monuments, to the significance of which Denmark awoke early. Care is bestowed equally upon thousands of prehistoric grave sites and dozens of historic castles. At the open-air museum outside Copenhagen have been assembled representative farmhouses and buildings from throughout the country, while in *Den gamle Staden* (the Old Town), the city council of Aarhus has rescued, transported and reconstructed properties worthy of conservation from the development areas of the city centre. Urban advance and renewal are visible processes. And since most development is coastal, among its frequently invisible consequences for Denmark has been maritime pollution. In particular, the sluggish waters of the Kattegat are sensitive to the increasing volume of effluent entering them.

The checks and balances that determine Danish developments are strongly centralized. The greatest happiness of the greatest number of Danes is theoretically assured by a Folketing elected by a system of proportional representation. There are nine parties, of which the Communists and Single-Taxers (legacy of Henry George) usually fail to hold seats. Social Democrats generally claim a safe majority over the combined membership of their two nearest rivals, the Liberal-Democrats and Conservatives. Most governments are coalitions. The Slesvig Party usually obtains one representative and there are two representatives each from the Faeroes and Greenland. Denmark is a politically alert country, urged to action by a vigorously independent press. Radicalism is tempered by conformity; seriousness, by a ready sense of humour.

It is the humour of the man in the street (doubly infectious to other Scandinavians because of the free use of the glottal stop) and the light touch with which the hard-driven 'merchant's harbour' (*København*) carries its problems that help to make Copenhagen Scandinavia's favourite capital. Problems are less intractable in an atmosphere where gastronomic indulgence is accepted, the aroma of cigar smoke is less heavily taxed, and alcohol is subject to fewer restraints than anywhere else in the North. Bonhomie and bohemianism are part and parcel of a city whose core breaks into such romantic examples of architecture as baroque Charlottenborg and rococo Amalienborg, where fortifications and moats are moulded into parks and pools and, free port apart, where wharves and quays have become waterfront promenades. For the summer visitor, in particular, so much of Copenhagen's life approaches a harlequinade by August Bournonville, founder of Danish ballet. Tivoli garden, neither beer garden nor bear garden, is one expression of it – by day a Kubla Khan pleasure dome, by night an Aladdin's cave. Its waltzes and polkas may not equal those of Vienna, but H. C. Lumbye and Knut Riisager have given to them their own popular and piquant musical styles. The Lutheran bells that call Denmark's cities to Sunday worship have a Latin leaven of chimes in the carillon of Copenhagen's town hall.

The appeal of Copenhagen also lies in its liberties. It is relaxed and uninhibited. The narrow winding streets of the university quarter, focusing on the Round Tower, are familiar with student protest. Beyond the classical restraints of the museum that houses Bertel Thorvaldsen's sculptures, the chinoiserie of the dragon-spired Bourse, the solid bulk of the Royal Theatre by Kongens Nytorv, where Ludvig Holberg's comedies still proclaim the rights of the common man, lies the sailors' quarter of Nyhavn. Morning, noon and night it echoes to the sound of bottle and glass, the throb of dance bands and the polyglot tongues of seafarers. It has a gaudy fairground atmosphere and the figures in its street scene are those of James Ensor. It was psychedelic before the word was invented: pornographic, before pornography was disguised by its classical name. Liberty may lead to licence – not least in the printed word, from which all restrictions have been removed – and it would be idle to pretend that Denmark lacks social diseases. Not surprisingly, social medicine and care claim correspondingly more attention.

Although Copenhagen's liberties are taken for granted, it has not always been so. There was a time when the seventeenth-century astronomer Tycho Brahe fled from the autocratic Christian IV, leaving Uraniborg observatory on the island of Hven for the freedom of Prague. Near where a fountain to the legendary Gefion recalls the origin of Denmark, the Museum of the German Occupation (1940–44) records the days when a spiritual darkness lay over the noontide land. The red and white Dannebrog, Europe's oldest flag, still flies at half-mast until noon on 9 April, the anniversary of the occupation, and the literature of the resistance is still remembered.

As with Vienna, Copenhagen has the feeling of a capital which has known more spacious times. Under the pressure of circumstance Denmark has contracted territorially. Yet Copenhagen retains a European stature. Again, Denmark has disposed of the fragments of its tropical outposts in India, Africa and Caribbea. Their ghosts are remembered (like Hamlet's father) in the halls of turreted Elsinore's museum. Yet Denmark thrives upon a web of trading connections with the tropics which is infinitely more complex and remunerative than it was during its imperial days. Danes suffer no illusions about the size and status of their country, yet experience enables them to think in a world context. Denmark cannot escape the strategic consequences of its location at the entrance to the Baltic and it is vulnerable for this reason. But it is also fortunate in that it profits from the fact that Copenhagen is the Baltic's largest and most enterprising entrepot.

There are historical legacies of responsibility, of which the two principal belong to high latitudes. The Faeroes and Greenland have little in common with Denmark proper and their problems have taxed the ingenuity of a people which has adopted a highly responsible attitude to them both. The Faeroe Islands, technically a county of Denmark and represented accordingly in its councils, are a loftier and bleaker archipelago than the Shetlands and Orkneys and lie 200 miles north of the latter. They are occupied by some 25,000 inhabitants whose fisher-farmer community is centred on Thorshavn. The resources of the Faeroes are unable to support a standard of living comparable to that of Denmark proper and their entire attitude to life and way of life differ so fundamentally from those of Denmark that it is hardly surprising to find strong separatist tendencies expressed. The distinctiveness of the Faeroese language and culture is increasingly acknowledged by Denmark.

The Faeroes lie on the traditional sea route from Scandinavia to Iceland and Greenland. Since the Hague International Court accepted Denmark's sovereignty over Greenland in 1921, a protectorate has been established over the scattered community of some 25,000 Eskimos. Most Eskimo settlements are on the west coast – the coast occupied in the Middle Ages by Norse colonists. The paternalistic Danish policy towards the Eskimo community, its rigorous exclusion of outsiders and the carefully managed monopoly of The Greenland Trading Company have provided a model for the treatment of a culturally retarded minority people. But Greenland's resources –

from minerals to fisheries – are drawn increasingly into the commercial orbit. In addition, the protection of the native minority becomes progressively more difficult with the multiplication of trans-polar air routes and the expansion of Thule as a staging post. Yet the problem must be kept in perspective for Greenland is larger than the whole of Scandinavia, so that the stream of tourist day trippers to the east coast from Reykjavik, the short-period summer expeditions by scientists, even the exploitation of the strictly limited mining concessions are unlikely to disturb seriously the land or its people. Scientifically and socially the Danes have done much for Greenland.

Denmark is a well-organized and well-maintained land, though the smiling landscape does not always imply a land of smiles. The high proportion of plump and pink people gives the impression of healthy minds in healthy bodies. Grundtvig's ideal of a land where 'few have too much and fewer too little' is near at hand. A sense of history and a feel for antiquity add depth to daily life. It is evident in the attitude to institutions such as the monarchy, democratized yet retaining among its picturesque trappings the Order of the Elephant; in such features as the sonorous Bronze Age trumpet, the *lur* – trade mark for butter since 1906, but also stirring overtones of Adam Oehlenschlager's poem of a golden age; in such conceits as the bucolic and pastoral engravings that take precedence over industrial and urban scenes on the reverse side of paper money. It is an attitude maintained side by side with a strong sense of the contemporary – inclining to the functional, admiring the comfortable, exuding the amiable. Out of a practical approach to everyday life has grown a new technical virtuosity: out of the appreciation of everyday things, a concern for critical detail.

Among the treasured manuscripts of the Royal Library in Copenhagen – beyond the vines and roses of its quiet garden – is that of Carl Nielsen's Third Symphony. It is a meticulous but modest-looking document which acquires new dimensions when translated into orchestral terms. Nielsen called it *Sinfonia expansiva*. It is a powerful, purposeful, thrusting work, born of a decade which stirred with new rhythms and strange harmonies. The title might well express Denmark's progress into the nuclear age of Niels Bohr.

6 Finland

SINCE THE FINNS arrived in their country during the first century AD both land and people have been characterized by a single word – isolation. Unlike their neighbours in Denmark, Norway and Sweden, the Finns took no part in the Viking excursions westward, eastward and southward. When Finland (*Suomi* to the Finns) became part of the kingdom of Sweden, it became also, sporadically, the field of Sweden's battles, but was otherwise merely a remote area of the realm. When, nearer to our own times, the Europeans took to tourism, they happily visited Norway and Sweden, but Finland, three or four days' journey from London or Paris, remained off the most lightly beaten track. In 1917, when Finland declared its independence, the new state was born without friends or allies. In 1945, twice defeated by the Soviet Union, its political isolation reached a new peak. As post-war Europe organized itself into blocs and alliances, Finland had to remain bravely alone, and was initially denied by the Soviet Union membership even of the United Nations.

In the past, geographical and political isolation has been paralleled by individual and personal isolation. The Finns have chosen to live, in the country, often far from each other, instead of clustering in villages; they have even sometimes feared any intrusion on their solitude. Their language, with its sharp individuality, has in part reinforced their remoteness. Yet in this isolation they have developed without self-pity; rather they have taken a certain pride in their loneliness and in the personal independence it has fostered. Today their long isolation has been diminished by the natural growth of towns, by the aeroplane and by shifting political movements. (That the first Strategic Arms Limitation Talks could have been held in Helsinki in 1969 would have seemed unbelievable twenty years earlier.) Yet the

Finns still bear the marks of a people cradled in solitude, and retain a distinctiveness in the context of the North as a whole.

In the Nordic family Finland has the status, in a sense, of a half-brother. The racial origins of the majority of the Finns are non-Scandinavian; and while the other four countries speak languages recognizably similar and to a large extent mutually understandable, Finnish is totally different. Various theories as to the origin of the Finns have been put forward and demolished, and no definitive evidence to support any single one has yet been found. The most likely homelands of the ancestral Finns seem to have been either south-central Russia or the south-east Baltic, where they certainly sojourned for a time before crossing to Finland. Their melodious language belongs to the Finno-Ugrian group, whose origins are equally controversial.

In looks and temperament the Finns have a certain non-Scandinavian strain. Many of them – the majority perhaps – could mingle unnoticed among Swedes and Danes and Norwegians. But probably not the Karelians from the east, who are so often made outstanding by their striking features or their liveliness of manner, or both. In temperament the Finns are often immediately identifiable by their greater imagination, spontaneity and enthusiasm, and their addiction to more extreme behaviour, whether for good or ill. Such extremes are expressed, for instance, in a loyalty in friendship rarely met elsewhere, and the kind of political volatility which helped to give Finland fifty different governments in its first fifty years of independence; in a considerable gift for large-scale organization contrasted with habits of drinking which prevent some of them from organizing so much as a mouse-trap.

The Finns have also had a rougher journey through history than their Scandinavian neighbours, chiefly because their country has been throughout the centuries recurrently buffeted by Sweden's wars or Russian oppression. The Finnish sense of nationhood has been accentuated by challenge, but at the same time it has been modified by the influence of the neighbouring states. Finland was part of the kingdom of Sweden from the twelfth century until 1809. From 1809 to 1917 it was a Grand Duchy of Russia. Thus over the course of more than six hundred years Finland acquired Swedish institutions – form of government, legal system, the Lutheran Church, and a similar way of life.

The Swedish language was brought by Swedish settlers and officials, and adopted by a certain number of Finns when it had become the official language of Finland. Today about 7 per cent of the population, mainly in the south and west, speak Swedish as their mother tongue, and Finland is officially a bilingual country. Moreover, since the early days of independence, official and semi-official ties between Finland and the other Scandinavian countries have grown continuously stronger, as has the entire westward orientation of the country.

The century during which Finland was a Grand Duchy of Russia was in retrospect a fruitful one, despite the recurring attempts at russification and oppression of its last twenty years or so. The country was in personal union with the tsar, whose powers were limited by the existing constitutional laws. Finland was internally autonomous, but was totally subject to Russia in its foreign relations. During this period, nevertheless, Finland replaced its outmoded Diet by the first unicameral Parliament in Europe, and became the first country in Europe to give women the vote (1906). In the cultural sphere the fruits were less easy to assess, but important to the Finns, with their lively interest in the arts. There were many contacts with St Petersburg, then just across the border, and the rich artistic life of nineteenth-century Russia added stimulus to Finnish ambitions. Nor were the opportunities of careers in the imperial military and civil services, in engineering and in commerce, neglected by the Finns.

Before the early post-war years, Finland was the least visited of the Scandinavian countries, and had retained a certain primitive appeal which air travel and modernization have still not completely dispelled. Today one can traverse much of the country by new motor roads, as fine as almost any in Europe, and stay in elegant and comfortable hotels on the edge of nowhere. But 'nowhere' remains, particularly in the east and north-east, a vast, beautiful and sparsely-inhabited area, where the interwoven pattern of lake and forest brings to a stop much human movement and most mechanized travel. This is the land of primeval forest, of the intoxicating springtime scent of birches and glades of lily of the valley, of the warm resinous smells of summer conifers, of wood smoke, of the faint odours of decay of autumn mushrooms. It is the land, too, of the magic and mystery to which the imaginative Finns respond so readily, and which is the source of so much of their folklore.

The Finnish and Swedish Baltic archipelagos form an almost continuous chain, and closely resemble each other. In this chain the major link is formed by the Åland Islands, Swedish-speaking but an autonomous province of Finland, and historically important beyond their size. Napoleon called them the key to Stockholm – a strategic truth which echoed uncomfortably in Swedish ears during and shortly after the Second World War. But while there are similarities of seascape between Sweden and Finland, the landscape of interior Finland is unique in Europe. More than sixty thousand lakes mean that one is rarely far from water. Forests covering seventy per cent of the country mean that wherever one looks, the eye falls somewhere on a dense and dark serrated mass of pine and spruce. In summer it is a gently rolling composition of blue and green; in winter a white and grey eternity where frozen lakes are hidden by the universal blanket of snow. In its silence and spaciousness it is tranquil, grave, sometimes melancholy, often monotonous. In general it lacks both scenic magnificence and intimate appeal. Yet it engenders nostalgia, and whenever the traveller returns to Finland he is struck anew by a beauty unusual and greater than he remembered.

Even in the loneliest wilderness the traveller will sometimes catch sight of the chimney of a paper mill, or see a great raft of bundled timber floating across a lake. For this very combination of forest and lake has formed the basis of the prosperity, in an international context, of a remote country. From the vast forests the Finns have for long exported timber and processed wood in all its forms, from matches through pulp to newsprint. The rivers and lakes have provided transport for timber laid on the ice before the spring thaw, eventually to reach its destination at a lakeside mill or southern port. The lake and river system has seemed right up to the present almost artfully contrived to carry Finland's principal raw material. Only in recent times has road transport become possible, more rapid and more economic for a large number of timber journeys.

The existence of forest and water has given Finland an industrial background different from that of most young countries. Commonly the first steps into industrialization are made by way of textile or similar manufactures, at first on a small scale and for the home market only. The wood-processing industry, by contrast, can exist only on a large scale, only if it keeps constantly up to date, and only if it has considerable export markets. Thus Finland has been forced to think on a bigger scale and to look far beyond the Baltic, working in dimensions unusual for a country with a population of less than five million. The Finns have been equal to the task. Sometimes, indeed, their obsession with sheer size can become slightly ludicrous. They have been helped by their recognition at an early stage that cut-throat competition for exports between several Finnish firms could do a small country no good, and that central selling organizations should take their place (as they have done in other branches of industry and agriculture). Such an arrangement may smack of the cartel, but international competition, on the whole, is often too fierce to allow price-fixing, and Finland tends to run into cyclical balance of payments problems as world paper prices fluctuate.

This experience of large-scale manufacture eased somewhat one of the greatest industrial efforts Finland has ever had to face – the payment of post-war reparations to the Soviet Union. As part of the peace settlement Russia demanded reparations, payable over six years, in the form of ships, locomotives, machinery, and even complete industrial plants. Finland at that time had only few and modest heavy engineering and metal industries. It had always been an importer of machines and machinery, and so had a dearth of trained engineers and skilled technicians. Yet, with characteristic tenacity, the Finns managed to build up these totally new industries and complete deliveries to the Soviet Union within the appointed time. More than that, they gave a determined positive turn to the situation. The Finnish economy, they rightly declared, had stood for too long on a single wooden leg; through the reparations demands they were able to balance it more securely on a second metal leg.

As a result the products of the metal and engineering industries now account for more than twenty-five per cent of Finnish exports. Finland has become particularly known for the excellence of its ice-breakers and paper-making machinery, having wisely concentrated on items within its own special experience. At the same time, the search for ore deposits has been intensified. After the war, Finland's resources were thought to be limited to fairly generous copper deposits, and a small supply of low-quality iron ore. Now Finland is mining in addition pyrites, zinc, nickel and various other minerals, and has become one of the world's largest producers of vanadium, used in steel manufacture. And there are geologists who suspect that the total range and supply of minerals may be far greater than is known at present. Concurrently, power supply has been considerably increased by harnessing the broad rivers and rapids of the northern part of the country, and by building large thermal power stations based upon imported oil. But supply barely keeps pace with the expansion of industry, and work has begun on the construction of a group of nuclear power stations in the south, where far more power is consumed than its own modest resources could provide.

Nuclear power is a far cry from the agricultural pattern of life which dominated the country from the Middle Ages until the Second World War. And although within a single generation the economy and way of life have been radically reorientated, farming still gives Finland, particularly outside the towns, its particular flavour and identity, its links with the past, and in some ways its anchorage in the present.

The Finns still think of themselves as a nation of countrymen, anxious to flee their cities whenever they can. There is still nothing incongruous in the fact that the President's neo-classical palace in Helsinki looks right on to a colourful and totally countrified market. It still remains hard for the Finns to accept the obvious facts that much of their harsh land is unsuited to agriculture, and that rationalization cannot be postponed indefinitely. This has already been delayed by the circumstances which followed the wars with the Soviet Union. If the conditions of the armistice favoured the development of industry, they held up the rationalization and reduction of agriculture. Finland had to cede to the USSR ten per cent of its land, mostly in the east, and including much of Karelia and the ancient town of Viipuri (Viborg); every eighth Finnish citizen lost his home and his livelihood, derived more often than not from the land. Resettlement of the farmers farther west was accomplished remarkably well, in social and human terms, but it increased the number of smallholdings by splitting up larger farms at a time when economics demanded the reverse.

Yet the Finns have wrought miracles out of their poor soil and hard climate, and made themselves more than self-sufficient in dairy products. This would not have been possible without the traditional alliance of forestry and agriculture. The golden rule has always been that every farmer should possess at least twice as much forest as field. The forest has provided both a cash crop, and work for master and men in winter. The remote, almost primitive smallholding and the modern automated paper-making plant are more closely related than would at first appear.

The smallholding has been in many ways the basis of Finnish society, and were it to disappear its influence would remain, at least for a time. The absence of a feudal system and the rarity of the tenant farmer have bred a nation of independent yeomen. The Finn today, whether farmer or industrial worker, is his own man, able to speak naturally and as an equal with all whom he may meet. Remoteness has also bred a taste for solitude and a gift for the making of entertainment, particularly in amateur drama and music. Most notably, it kept alive longer than in almost any other European country the traditions of oral poetry, perpetuated over the centuries by word of mouth. *Kalevala*, Finland's folk epic, was committed to paper only in the nineteenth century, although much of it may have existed for about a thousand years. And the last of the great rune-singers, with their prodigious memories, died only early this century.

Solitude and isolation have probably nourished the imagination and creative gifts of the Finns, who constantly return to the countryside for inspiration. But they hardly explain the vitality and energy which have brought about, particularly since the end of the war, a creative explosion. This was set off in part by the national and individual need to maintain the country's identity in the shadow of the Soviet Union. The same need had been felt during the Russian oppression of the last years of the nineteenth century and the early years of this century. Then the music of Jean Sibelius, Eero Järnefelt, Leevi Madetoja and Toivo Kuula sounded a rallying call to national consciousness. Partly for this reason Sibelius especially has often been categorized as a national romantic, although he regarded himself as a classicist. Certainly for the Finns above all his music evokes the varying moods of the landscape they so much love.

The Finns respect and reverence their artists to a point sometimes the other side of idolatry (but have no such regard for their politicians). This climate of opinion, combined with the emergence from time to time of a great or outstanding figure, or a great work, seems to stimulate creative activity and confidence. Sibelius has been followed by a number of composers of talent remarkable in relation to the population. After Eliel Saarinen (1873–1950) and Alvar Aalto (b. 1898) have come a similarly disproportionate number of outstanding architects, many of whom, notably Wiljö Rewell (1910–64), have worked outside Finland. In the applied arts there has been an extra-ordinary upsurge, and an urge to re-design almost every item in daily use. In literature and painting quantity has tended to surpass quality, although the literary situation is one of considerable interest. Until the early nineteenth century, Swedish was the language of the schools and the printing presses, as well as of government and the law. But Finnish, with its unusual wealth and subtlety of vocabulary, was the spoken language of the people, and the language of the lore and legends preserved and transmitted orally from one generation to another. When *Kalevala*, collected and assembled by Elias Lönnrot, was published in 1835, it touched the veins of both poetry and nationalism. J. L. Runeberg (1804–77) was a nationalist poet, though he wrote in Swedish; so did the many-sided Zachris Topelius (1818–98) who taught the Finns about their country as poet, novelist, historian, newspaper editor and university professor. Aleksis Kivi (1834–72) was the first great prose writer and dramatist to use the Finnish language, and his novel *Seven Brothers* has become a national classic. A later novelist, F. E. Sillanpää (1888–1964) was a Nobel prize-winner; among contemporary novelists whose work is known out-side Finland in translation are Mika Waltari (b. 1908), author of *Sinuhe the Egyptian*, and Väinö Linna (b. 1920), who made his reputation with his war novel *The Unknown Soldier*. Today the Finns claim, as do the Icelanders, that they are the world's biggest buyers – or readers – of books; certainly their excellent bookshops and libraries, whether in cities or small villages, give substance to this claim.

In painting, as in music, architecture and literature, the national romantic movement was the mainspring of creativity, particularly in the case of Akseli Gallen-Kallela (1865–1931), who is known above all for his paintings of subjects drawn from *Kalevala*. Gallen-Kallela has been called the first modern Finnish painter. Contemporary with him, but more universally modern, was Hélène Schjerfbeck (1862–1945). Her exceptional talent developed uninfluenced by the national romantic movement, and she was eventually recognized as a pioneer and reformer of Finnish art. There has followed a large number of artists who, despite their gifts, have failed to create a specifically Finnish school, or to make a distinctive contribution to modern European painting as a whole. On the other hand Finland can count a number of excellent and individual sculptors, among them two of international stature. Väinö Aaltonen (1894–1966) was a pioneer in his time, working with particular success in the native granite; the much younger Eila Hiltunen (b. 1922) has distinguished herself as a welding sculptor, working almost entirely in metal, in which she has produced figures remarkable for their fluidity and movement. Hers is also the immense and now famous Sibelius memorial, an abstract composition made entirely of welded steel pipes.

Finland has produced, and continues to produce, a disproportionate number of artists in every sphere because it is also a country of enthusiastic amateurs. The Finns provide fairly substantial patronage and financial backing for professional artists, and they also constantly seek outlets for their own creative gifts, whether in amateur dramatic groups and local orchestras, or in the more solitary pursuits of writing and painting. Enthusiasm may sometimes distort judgement, but it makes it possible for the artist to work in an atmosphere of particular freedom.

But today, in the visual sphere, Finland is known abroad above all for its architects. Alvar Aalto, a man of deep human insight, humour and humility, is one of the handful of great architects in the world today. He sums up his philosophy of architecture in the simple formula: 'H is more important than S.' (H = the human factor; S = the system.) In the early thirties he had already established himself as a master of the modern idiom, in the best sense of the expression. From the late forties onward he showed more and more his brilliant combination of the organic and the inventive; so that his buildings can stimulate and delight without evoking either shock or surprise. He has mastered that most difficult of all tasks – the harmonizing of a modern building with the vast Finnish landscape which surrounded it, and of making modern man feel equally at home in a large concrete structure as in the forest. Aalto has done a great deal of work outside Finland, in countries as far apart, in space and temperament, as the USA and Italy. Unlike many Finnish artists in other spheres, he does not depend for inspiration or success on his native soil. His work is organic and harmonious whatever its setting.

Many of the younger generation of architects have studied under Aalto. It says much for both master and pupils that they have not imitated him, but learnt from him to invent within a human framework. Possibly from him they have also acquired the elements of that confidence without which civilized architecture cannot exist. Their success in the design of modern churches – that searching test of spirit as well as of mind and technique – is in itself witness to their confidence. Some of these new churches are externally daunting; but their interiors, however unorthodox and removed from tradition, are informed by a certainty of spirit and a breadth of faith which, whether formally Christian or not, rarely fail to move even the un-believer who visits them out of nothing more than curiosity.

The Finns are immensely proud of their architects, whose work is more fully discussed in the press and among the people than is architecture in most other countries. Pride and discussion in turn stimulate an awareness of surroundings which has made some of Finland's newer towns outstandingly beautiful. Tapiola, outside Helsinki, has become world-famous; but there are others where, for instance, a new civic centre and a general face-lift have given the citizens fresh satisfactions and stemmed, at least in part, the drift to the south-west. For this is Finland's great problem, as agriculture dimin-ishes in importance, and as the countryman comes to town. The south-west has the industrial towns and the money: Tampere (Tammerfors), the second town in Finland, home of the textile industry; Turku (Åbo), with its port, only slightly smaller, before 1812 the Finnish capital and made charming by its graceful neo-classical buildings; Lahti, young and vigorous, specializing in furni-ture-making; and the ports of Pori (Björneborg) on the Gulf of Bothnia, and Kotka and Hamina (Fredrikshamn) on the Gulf of Finland. And, of course, Helsinki (Helsingfors), the increasingly powerful magnet, the port and capital set between woodland, sea and islands.

Helsinki is sometimes called 'the white city of the North', and so it appears as one approaches it from the sea. In reality the only truly white building is the neo-classical cathedral, which, with its copper dome, dominates the skyline. The cathedral and the beautifully proportioned yellow and pastel-tinted buildings which surround it are the result of a felicitous collaboration, in the early eighteen-hundreds, between the native town-planner, J. A. Ehrenström, and the German-born architect Carl Ludvig Engel.

They gave to the official core of the city a dignity, on a modest scale, possessed by few European capitals. Ehrenström and Engel planned only for the small peninsular site then sufficient to contain Helsinki's population of four thousand. Today, with more than half a million inhabitants, it has sprawled into the hinterland and leap-frogged to the neighbouring islands, and the conflicting pulls of centrifugal and centripetal forces have already made themselves felt. The Finns foresaw this conflict, but despite their efforts, failed to prevent it. They attempted to create in Tapiola a town with sufficient industries to make it at least partly self-contained. But Tapiola is only six miles from Helsinki, and proved highly magnetic to commuters and hardly at all to industrialists. After Tapiola, there followed suburbs, each to house four or five thousand people, and not more than half an hour's journey from Helsinki. Again, industry was invited, provided it was clean and quiet, and polluted neither air nor water – so the response was inevitably small. The dormitory areas east and west of Helsinki can be reached only by road, over bridges linking the islands which turn into bottlenecks at peak hours. The ensuing congestion led to the decision to build an underground rail-way, though with overwater bridges, to ease life for commuters. And so the city once made so delightfully livable by its compactness and its enchanting mixture of town, country and seascape, began to assume the problems and character, in part, of other big cities all over the world, where underground railways are certain heralds of the triumph of technology over humanity.

Over against the forces of dispersal stands Alvar Aalto's near-visionary plan to give Helsinki a new centre. Aalto is an imaginative town-planner as well as an architect; he is convinced that the bigger a city grows, the more important it becomes that its citizens should be able to meet, in their leisure time, in a fairly compact central area. His new centre, near and alongside a pleasant stretch of water, would include a theatre or an opera house, an art gallery, a public library, a concert hall and a 'congress building' – the last a city hall for enter-tainment rather than administrative purposes. Aalto's plan has neither been accepted nor ruled out in its entirety. Only a conference hall and the 'congress building' have been undertaken so far, and com-pletion of the whole plan rests in the realm of hope rather than intention.

Despite rapid development and widespread rebuilding, Helsinki still manages to keep some contact with nature. One is still rarely far from either the woodlands or the sea, with its innumerable creeks, bays and inlets. The Finns are by temperament conservationists, whose concern for natural features is such that they will build a flight of steps round a tree rather than cut the tree down. They have been fairly successful, up to date, in preventing Helsinki's fragmented coastline from being swallowed by concrete, and one feels that, as long as they can persist in this frame of mind, the capital need never become totally urbanized. Another escape from urbanization is provided by some of the inshore islands which have been put to a special purpose. The best-known is Suomenlinna, the island fortified in the eighteenth century to defend Helsinki, and now a museum piece. The zoo and the open-air museum occupy two other islands left in their natural state, and somehow even the short voyage by ferry between mainland and islands heightens the sense of both occasion and escape.

The Finns are now making a determined attempt to prevent Helsinki's population from increasing much above half a million. Some years ago the setting up of new industries in the capital was banned, and now various industrial concerns, including Finland's oldest sugar refinery, have been moved from the capital to outlying areas. So, up to the present, the people of Helsinki can be judged to have achieved the best of both worlds, with sailing, swimming and ski-ing at their back door, and theatres, concerts and restaurants at their front door. Nine well-patronized theatres keep them in touch with the main currents of European drama, classical and contemporary, as well as the output of their own native playwrights. There are likewise enough concerts to bring to their ears music both established and experimental – the latter fully provided by the large band of younger Finnish composers. Finnish opera has produced singers of international reputation, among them Aulikki Rautawaara, Anita Välkki, Kim Borg and Martti Talvela.

Many of the provincial towns have theatres, restaurants and communal activities which satisfy their inhabitants. The real gulf now is between the townsman and the countryman, and in particular, the countryman cut off by distance or water from a town of substance. Even the islands relatively near to Helsinki are losing their small populations as discontent with the absence of shops, restaurants and cinemas sets in. The northern half of the country and the north-east in particular are becoming more remote psychologically, though the excellent domestic air services make them less so physically. Decentralization is a topic in which few are personally interested. Industrialists have no wish to leave the south, with its greater amenities, for the less economically rewarding north. One positive step has been the establishment at Oulu, on the Gulf of Bothnia, of the most northerly university in the world; another, the building of a state-sponsored steel works at Raahe, not far away. But it is difficult to envisage the achievement of anything approaching equilibrium between north and south.

Planning on a national scale comes hard to the Finns, whose political notions tend to be dominated by sectional interests, and whose governments often appear to function on moving staircases. Finland elects by proportional representation every four years. Since 1944 no party has achieved more than 56 of the total 200 seats in the single-chamber parliament; therefore coalitions, with their inevitable horse-trading between parties, have been the rule. The three largest parties, which each tend to collect, with variations, roughly a quarter of the votes, have been the Centre (formerly Agrarian), Communist and Social-Democratic parties; the Conservative, Liberal and Swedish Parties have shared the rest of the votes. In 1970, however, the Communists gained only 36 seats, against the 37 won by the Conservatives. So, since the war Finland has been governed mainly by a 'Red-Green' coalition; that is, a Social-Democratic-Agrarian alliance. In Finland, as in other Northern countries, the former Agrarian Party has become gradually urbanized. After a period in which many of its members were termed 'asphalt Agrarians' by their opponents, it changed its name to the 'Centre Party', as did the other Scandinavian Agrarian Parties. Between 1948 and 1966 the Communists, whatever their strength, were excluded, no other party being willing to work with them. However, in 1966 they were taken, together with the Social Democratic and Centre Parties, into a government which commanded three-quarters of the votes in Parliament. The Finnish Communists had moderated their views considerably, and in office honoured their promise to work within the democratic framework. Moreover, this government showed unexpected stability, and was able to handle the economic situation with considerable success. Thus after the 1970 elections, despite the shift of votes to the right, a Social-Democrat-Centrist-Communist government was again formed. But by then a hardening of attitudes inside the Communist party had led to tensions in this tripartite coalition. Internal strife developed between the Stalinist hardliners and the moderates; and in the spring of 1971 the Communists left the government.

Since Finland's inception as a sovereign state, the Finns have placed the task of assuring stability on the shoulders of their presidents. The powers accorded to the man they elect as president are considerable. He plays a key role in both domestic and foreign policy, and in view of the always delicate nature of Finno-Soviet relations, he carries a particularly heavy responsibility. It is Finland's great good fortune to have had, since the Finno-Soviet armistice of 1944, three presidents whose approach to relations with the Soviet Union has been on the whole consistent, calm and firm.

At the end of the war the Finns chose as president their military hero Marshal Mannerheim. This aristocratic figure, who had fought the revolutionaries in the Civil War of 1918, and the Soviets in the wars of 1939–40 and 1941–44, had nevertheless always counselled moderation in Finland's dealings with the Soviet Union. He had a powerful ally in the Prime Minister, J. K. Paasikivi, who became President in 1946, when Mannerheim resigned on grounds of ill-health.

Paasikivi, who held the reins for ten years, brought Finland into a more stable relationship with the Soviet Union than many had thought possible. He insisted from the outset that the prime duty of the Finns was to secure the confidence of the Soviet Union, and to assure it that their country would at no time be used as the base for an attack on Russia. To the outsider, this sounded a simple enough formula. In fact, it ran totally counter to the Soviets' deeply-rooted suspicion of Finland, and to Finland's centuries-old hatred of the Russia of both Tsars and Soviets. Paasikivi's policy succeeded, and has been continued by his successor, U. K. Kekkonen. The result is a relationship in which the Finnish people live in complete democratic freedom, while the government must avoid actions likely to arouse Soviet suspicions. Finnish governments are now considerably more free than they were in the immediate post-war decade; but it remains essential for them to consider all moves in foreign policy in the light of the possible Soviet reaction. Soviet interference has been confined to the occasional demonstration, as if to remind the Finns of their obligations. But by and large, the Finns are already well enough aware of their position for such demonstrations to be fairly rare. And no visitor to Finland could today detect any direct Soviet influence on the life of the country, simply because it does not exist. Moreover, President Kekkonen has been able to give to the neutrality imposed on Finland a more positive turn, although he has not always succeeded in carrying the other Scandinavian countries with him.

The Soviet presence on the eastern border ultimately decides Finland's destiny, and because it decides Finland's destiny, it influences the future of the other Scandinavian countries. In a world where politics and economics overlap, and economic blocs become as important as political alliances, even Finland's freedom to trade with whom it will is to some extent limited by its commercial treaty with the Soviet Union. The Finns recognize the limitations placed upon them from without. They can accept them, practised as they are in isolation, and tried by the rough road of their history.

7   Iceland

ICELAND (*Island* to the Icelanders), the most detached country in Europe, is among those that have gone through the greatest amount of change in the shortest time. It is only forty years since it was four or five days' rough sail from Copenhagen. The rugged adventure land is now only two hours' flight from Scotland, and a natural stop-over between the Old World and the New. Domestically, Iceland leapt into the air age from the horse age. It bypassed the railway, paid respect to the internal combustion engine and awaited jet propulsion. At the time when it celebrated the thousandth birthday of its Althing (or Parliament) in 1930, and even when it declared its final independence from Denmark in 1944, its transformation had only just begun. As with northern Scandinavia at large, it has benefited to a disproportionate degree from the introduction of new equipment and techniques; though paradoxically, the innovations that have hastened its material improvement and the forces that have facilitated its constitutional independence have carried with them the seeds of a new dependence.

Iceland, like Norway, is a lofty land. Its desolate plateaux have been born of fire out of water. Fire is still producing new land (pl. 9): water, wearing away the old. Nowhere in Europe is volcanicity more evident. Iceland has had more than twenty volcanoes active in historic time. It has hot springs by the hundred and steamfields (or to give them a more exotic name, solfataras) by the dozen. It is also a land subject to earthquakes, and the areas most favoured by human settlement coincide with those most susceptible to their effects. Structurally speaking, Iceland consists of layer upon layer of lava which has flowed intermittently through millennia of time. The older lava series rise in tabular masses several thousands of feet in height from the coastal flats. Their cliff-like sides, festooned with screes, are grey, black tulip or charcoal according to the play of light upon them – forbidding *côtes de nuit* on which little vegetation finds foothold. The younger lava outpourings – their turbulent writhings cooled into fantasies – are of dimensions more comprehensible to the human eye. In the drier north-east, ash deserts yield to wind-blown sand and gravel wastes: in the moister south-west, to deep bogs, on which the bog cotton waves and around which the golden troilus flourishes.

The austere grandeur of Iceland is exaggerated by treelessness and grasslessness. The landscape has a Mongolian baldness – a quality inseparable from the erosive work of what the saga literature called the Frost Giants. Baldness is exaggerated by the extensive icefields, fed by the moist Atlantic winds from the south-west, their equilibrium disturbed by the slightest changes in long-term temperature conditions. Only at favoured places, principally upon the marine and river terraces, are there tolerable soils for farming. Although the coastlands claim most of the more habitable lands, they too have their share of wild and barren areas – among them, the fjords of the north-west and the great *sandur* or sandy ice-edge plains that fringe Vatnajökull in the south. And all of these features are seen through an atmosphere subject to swift changes – the obscurities of storm, fog and winter darkness alternating with periods of strange luminosity or remarkable clarity. Snow-capped Snæfell, hanging in the sky like a Fujiyama seventy miles across Faxa Bay, is one criterion of visibility.

People have turned their backs on the barren interior of Iceland and, apart from concentration in a limited number of towns, have established a dispersed settlement around the coast. As in Norway, the detached family farm dominates, with frequent continuity of occupation since Viking times. The isolation of Iceland itself is consequently repeated in the isolation of most farmsteads. These facts have naturally influenced the behaviour and attitudes of Icelanders. Changes in attitudes have not kept pace with the changes in communications that have reduced the effects of distance. And, even assuming Iceland had not a language which has stood remarkably still while the languages of the rest of Norden have been subject to fundamental change, the thinking of its people would naturally be distinguished from the attitudes of Danes, Norwegians and Swedes because of its size, situation and status. Determinism may be an unfashionable doctrine, but a cold temperate climate (from which there is neither regional nor seasonal escape) and a frustrated development have inevitably bred neuroses in many Icelanders. Eternal vigilance in the face of natural hazards is balanced by jealous regard for all that touches upon the nation. Not surprisingly, Iceland has an almost love-hate relationship with more favoured lands in general, and with those upon which it depends in particular.

Icelanders are thin upon the ground. They have never been very thick, but in the twentieth century there have been more of them than at any time since the Middle Ages, when the figure is presumed to have reached about 70,000. Iceland's population has fluctuated greatly, and because of the continuity of its records, numbers can be more readily estimated than in most countries. There are still only 200,000 people occupying an area about the same size as Ireland. It is claimed that if all the people who had ever lived in Iceland were assembled together, they would not greatly exceed a million.

After the medieval golden age, Pelion was piled on Ossa (or Snæfell on Hekla) in the succession of misfortunes that afflicted the island. To the toll of the sea and of the recurrent natural disasters with their accompanying famines were added plagues and the inhibiting commercial effects of the Danish trading monopoly. If the ancient Norse had not conceived Ragnarök, the doom of the world, Icelandic imagination might have invented it. By 1801 the population had fallen to 47,000 and its physical and mental energies had been sapped. Emigration fever was to aggravate the situation. The fickle shoals of the sea and the uncertain harvests from the land impart continuing instability to the economy, but a new security now characterizes society. For most, the hardships of rural life described in the realist fiction of Gudmundur Magnusson, Gunnar Gunnarsson and Halldor Laxness, have also been softened. Population has multiplied responsively. Today, Iceland has the highest birthrate of any of the Nordic countries, while life expectancy is second only to that of Norway.

Iceland looks first to the sea for its wealth; but the way in which it approaches the resources of the sea has changed greatly in the twentieth century. Features of the old subsistence economy persist locally, but the fisheries require increasingly heavy capital investment in an up-to-date fleet of vessels. The fish catch consists principally of herring, with cod and haddock following. Its fishing grounds, as those of Norway, are on the continental shelf that surrounds the island. They are rich, but not inexhaustible. Throughout history, they have been a cause of international conflict. They remain so today. Since 1961 a twelve-mile fishing limit has girdled Iceland and trespass within it occasions diplomatic notes – even international incidents. Iceland would even like the limit extended to fifty miles.

Fishing techniques have improved so greatly that over-fishing is imminent. The volume of the catch increases not least because fishing has become a year-round instead of a seasonal pursuit. The importance of the fisheries to Iceland is such that they constitute nine-tenths of its exports by value. The catch is increasingly processed before export. Iceland's old-established stockfish, saltfish, klipfish, pickled herring, cod liver oil and herring meal are complemented by the products of refrigeration and fish-packing plants. Whaling is a residual pursuit, though a catch exceeding several hundreds is rare during the limited hunting season. The symbols of Renaissance cartography live again when the occasional spouting whale is juxtaposed with the backdrop of billowing smoke rising from Surtsey, Iceland's youngest volcano.

Although Icelanders live off the sea they are rooted in the land. Historically the land has provided meagre returns. Accordingly, beyond the pocket-handkerchief infields of the home farm, the farmer has ranged extensive outlands for hunting, fishing and fowling as well as pasturing. It is ironical that at a time when, through technical advance, Iceland's countryside is able to support more people at a higher standard of living, the drift from it has gathered momentum. Today only about 15 per cent of Iceland's population looks to farming for a living. By comparison with former times Iceland flows with milk if not with honey, though commercial use of land is difficult beyond those areas where collection and marketing is easy. In contrast to most of Scandinavia – the Faeroes apart – Iceland is a country of sheep rather than of cattle. Shepherding on the extensive common grazings presents picturesque features, with the pony generally retaining its traditional role over mechanized transport. Numbers of sheep fluctuate cyclically and seasonally. Winter-fed stock (about 400,000) may be only half of the summer numbers. Wool, always the basis of domestic industries, now supplies knitwear factories, while dressed sheepskins provide a distinctive export in their own right. A mutton cuisine complements a cod cuisine on the gastronomic front, though the variety of dishes that can be produced from either is strictly limited.

Extensive though Iceland may be, its stock-carrying capacity has been low. Over-stocking undoubtedly played a part in reducing the natural vegetation of Iceland during the early years of the settlement. The contemporary extension and improvement of the barbed-wired infield – by levelling, stoning, draining, fertilizing and rotational cropping – have provided an adequate and reliable fodder supply for the first time in Iceland's history. Tractor-operated machinery breaks a silence hitherto reserved for the sounds of nature. Although machines have increasingly replaced horses in field operations, the Icelandic pony (measured in thumbs rather than hands) retains importance for export and for recreation. The National Museum in Reykjavik, paying heed to art and archeology, to domestic crafts and the fisheries, also devotes a corner to the harness and saddlery of a creature inseparable from the life and customs of the nation.

The produce of the farmer is collected, processed and marketed according to the best Scandinavian methods. The first farmers' co-operative was established in 1882, since when there have emerged co-operative dairies, slaughterhouses, tanneries, meat-packing and fish-packing plants. The marketing of greenhouse produce is also co-operatively organized. Vegetables and flowers nursed beneath acres of glass in an atmosphere warmed by the waters of hot springs are tended by some of Iceland's most skilled workers in some of its most agreeable working conditions. Yet even here the shadows of surplus production and rising costs hang over the producer. Accordingly, Icelandic farmers strengthen their interests through a Farmers' Union (1945) while an Agricultural Production Board endeavours to plan production in relation to demand.

It is some measure of the transformation of Iceland that manufacturing and services now claim the greatest number of Iceland's employed population. Home-market industries, though in general small in scale, are varied in kind. Large enterprises such as the cement plant at Akranes which works shell beds for lime are unusual. This is partly because of the absence of raw materials in Iceland. The Swiss-sponsored aluminium plant at Straumsvik imports its raw materials, as must also Iceland's first oil refinery.

Such plants, as with the new tempo of life evident in the country at large, are inseparable from the harnessing and distribution of energy resources. Although the fisherman and farmer still depend basically upon imported oils, Iceland's energy derives increasingly from hydro-electric power. The island has some of Scandinavia's richest sources of natural energy, though only their fringes are tapped. The first major scheme to be developed was on the Sog river system: the second, at Burfell, on the Thjorsá river, also in the south-west. Eyes gloat over the potential of Dettifoss (with its broad forty-metre-high fall) and Gullfoss, but they are also tourist attractions as much likely to be protected as to be exploited by the National Power Company. At the same time, Iceland has untouched sources of thermal energy in its steamfields. Meanwhile electricity has been brought to nearly 95 per cent of the country's inhabitants.

Despite its thousand years of history Iceland has a raw rather than a mellow appearance. There is little softening around the edges of the forbiddingly grand natural scene. This is inseparable from two facts. The first is the absence of easily manipulated and durable building materials. Driftwood around the coast, glacial boulders and sod were basic to most structures until replaced by deal boards from Scandinavia and corrugated iron. Concrete now prevails. The engineer rejoices in it for bridges, waterfronts and hydro-electric installations; the civic authorities, for public buildings and housing; the Lutheran church, for the new centres of worship that would gladden the heart of the patron saint Thorlak. The second fact is that the hard outlines of the usually colour-washed buildings are rarely softened by any vegetation. The native birch and exotic rowan rarely rise to the second storey. Overhead cables and telephone wires, underfoot dirt roads (even on the outskirts of the capital) impart something of the atmosphere of Canadian prairie settlements to the more concentrated Icelandic communities. Picturesqueness and cosiness are not qualities possessed by the Icelandic landscape.

The most remarkable human development in Iceland has been the rise of Reykjavik. Within living memory the capital was no more than a large village. Despite the rustic charms with which the French water colourist Paul Gaimard invested it, the succession of distinguished visitors for whom Reykjavik was a landfall – Lord Dufferin, Sir Richard Burton, Richard Hooker, William Morris and Lord Bryce among others – generally described it in unflattering terms. Facets of its growth appear in *The Annals of Brekkukot* (1957), a novel by the Nobel prize winner, Halldor Laxness. Today, with its tributary area, Reykjavik has a population approaching 100,000. Only Akureyri in the far north, with some 10,000, has more than a tithe of the

capital's population. Keflavik (*c.* 5,000) on the south-western peninsula of Reykjanes, Akranes (*c.* 4,000) across the bay from the capital,
and the harbour of Vestmanna-eyjar (the Westman Isles) are enlarged
villages by comparison with the towns of most countries. Reykjavik
is a powerful magnet for the young whose moods and rituals it reflects.

Centralization of function has been a necessary accompaniment of
the development of Iceland. Through Reykjavik Iceland is able to
assert and express itself. Trade and administration are concentrated in
it. Strangely enough, it lacks a deep-water harbour and jolly boats are
busy when cruise ships or cruisers put in. In the modest little Althing
building sixty members of parliament ring changes of coalition
between the four parties that are elected every four years. Although
there is a bicameral system, a single united chamber can be called if
required. The executive power is vested in a president and six or
seven cabinet ministers. The so-called Independence Party, pledged
to liberal trading and free enterprise, is the largest party, the principal
opposition to which comes from the Progressive Party. Splinter
groups have conducted minority agitations against membership of
NATO and the retention of the American base at Keflavik. There is
a strong feeling for a neutral line in world affairs. It is manifest in the
fact that the official *Handbook of Iceland* has no section on defence.
Icelanders are well aware of the strategic location of their island
which, in the flight paths of international air routes, is no longer to be
viewed in simple high-latitude terms of reference. Louis MacNeice's
'vertiginous crow's nest of the north' is an outmoded metaphor.

In all relationships, the number of inhabitants and the size of the
country are fundamental. Internationally, the comparative costs of
maintaining consular and diplomatic services and of representation
at international organizations is heavy. Domestically, the cry for
improved communications is ceaseless. Much was done by British
and American forces during the war to improve the road network,
and heavy investment has taken place in it since. Only a subsidized state
steamship company can afford to circumnavigate Iceland and link
together harbours that cannot be supplied by other means of transport. Only during the post-war period has it been possible to construct and maintain a system of lighthouses in any way approaching
the adequate. A complete telephone network is a service taken for
granted by even the remotest farmsteads, but costs of maintenance
(as for those of electricity distribution) are inordinately high. The

problems of providing services are comparable to those of Scandinavia's Nordkalotten. But at least the services of the northern areas of Norway, Sweden and Finland can be partly subsidized by the larger and more affluent population that lives in the south. Iceland, lacking any territory comparable to their southlands, is wholly equivalent to their Nordkalotten.

Communications are eased at the personal level. The network of personal relationships is closely drawn. Everyone seems to know or to know of everyone else. Understanding is the easier because of a society more economically egalitarian than anywhere else in Scandinavia and because of the widespread feeling for both the spoken and the written word. Latin never played the same part in literary expression as in most European countries: the vernacular has always predominated. Although language restricts the circulation of Icelandic books, the per capita number of titles published annually exceeds those for the rest of Scandinavia and approaches world leadership. Reykjavik's bookshops (like those of Helsinki) would put to shame those of many major cities of the English-speaking world. While research at the National University (founded in 1911) is dominated by the demands of the applied arts and sciences, philological investigation excites an interest beyond the campus. Isolation has protected the language so that Icelandic retains a storehouse of words of fundamental interest to students of Indo-European philology at large. Iceland's bookish interests have expanded immeasurably since the foundations of the National Library were laid by the Danish philologist C. C. Ravn in the early nineteenth century. For long its manuscript collections consisted mostly of photographs of treasures in other Scandinavian libraries, but the donation of part of Arni Magnusson's remarkable Copenhagen collection of early manuscripts was set in motion by the Danish government and they were sent to the University of Reykjavik in April 1971. In general, language and literature assume greater significance for the Icelanders because of their relatively limited material inheritance.

At the same time external symbols of national identity have been fostered – the flag, the National Anthem (1874), the national dress that is still regularly worn by older women, the 'Galahad-Viking' statuary (as W. H. Auden mischievously described it). More prestigious and expensive institutions have been established in recent years. Illustrative of them are a national museum, a national theatre, a symphony orchestra, naturally a state radio (founded in 1930 and among world leaders in the transmission of parliamentary debates) and shrines such as the studio homes of artists who have produced nationally significant paintings and sculptures.

Many of the externals of modern nations are urban-based rather than country-based. Iceland's culture is fundamentally rural. Its personality reposes in the silences and solitudes of its uninhabited wastes and in the unsophisticated character of its country people. Iceland's urban centres are not old enough to have developed a culture of their own. The traditional pleasures of church and chess, wrestling and pony racing, even of swimming (in the splendid hot baths) and athletics (in the excellent arenas) are inadequate to fill a void into which elements of alien cultures have rushed. Side by side with the invaluable mass-produced American mechanical and technical devices – not least automobiles which are the best possible for Icelandic conditions – have come the film, television (for the NATO base) and tourists (with consumer demands that set fashions in their own right). Though the USSR cannot compete with these, it makes forceful attempts to woo Iceland on the commercial front. It is difficult for Iceland either to absorb or to reject these influences and controls. Its new-found nationalism must be reconciled with them.

Iceland remains one of Europe's curiosities, both from the physical and human points of view. Each generation breeds an increasing number of potential enthusiasts who seek to explore and explain its natural phenomena. Iceland as a human phenomenon has equally compelling drama, and explanation of the successive acts that lead to the contemporary dénouement has bred its own schools of speculation. It was something of a miracle that early Norse colonists (let alone the Celtic anchorites who preceded them) contrived to reach the land, to occupy it and, with the bare bones of a primitive technology, to nurture their own distinctive civilization in the midst of such a savage wilderness. It was the legacy of its medieval scribes that led European scholars to rediscover this 'waste, chaotic battlefield of Frost and Fire' in the age of nineteenth-century romanticism and, in the process, to prompt Iceland to rediscover itself. The rediscovery was inseparable from scholars such as Gudbrandur Vigfusson, who helped to transmit the enthusiasm and respect that foreign academics had for his native country and thereby to foster in it a new confidence; from applied scientists and businessmen, who realized the practical importance for

Icelandic development of the mechanical revolution; from artists, such as Ásgrimur Jónsson, who helped his countrymen to see their land with new eyes. In the space of three generations, Icelanders have taken possession of their land anew – politically, culturally, economically. Nationalism may have been the primary impulse behind the success of modern Iceland, but the influence of the remote secular rhythms of the physical world can never be disregarded. Would this community on the margins of the habitable world have been transformed so speedily and so fundamentally if imponderables such as a short-term climatic improvement had not coincided with the most stimulating intellectual and technical episode in its history since the Middle Ages ?

18, 19 *Left:* The twelfth-century stave church at Borgund, Norway. Such churches, constructed from wood on the same skeletal principles as Gothic cathedrals, were common in Northern Europe in the early Middle Ages, but few examples still remain outside Norway. *Below:* The Henie-Onstad Gallery, near Oslo, designed by Jon Eikvar and Sven-Erik Engebretsen, expresses the contemporary mood.

20–23 Old and new in Sweden and Finland. *Opposite, above:* The Wennergren Centre for scientific research, Stockholm; architects, Sune Lindström and Als Bydén. *Opposite, below:* Kalmar Castle in Sweden, built in the twelfth century, and transformed in great splendour during the Vasa period. *Right:* The bell-tower of Porvoo (Sw. Borgå) Cathedral, Finland, dating from the fifteenth century. *Below:* Housing designed by Alvar Aalto in the nineteen-thirties for employees of the Sunila (Finland) cellulose factory.

24 Amalienborg, the Copenhagen palace of the Danish royal family, was built by the architect Niels Eigtved, 1749–60. It contains what has been described as one of the finest rococo squares in Europe.

25–27 *Above:* The new bridge across the Little Belt, connecting Funen and Jutland, was opened in 1970. More than a mile long, it is for motor traffic only. Architects, Peter Hvidt and O. Molgaard Nielsen. *Left:* old Icelandic farm buildings, made of grass-covered sods and corrugated iron, contrast with the modern concrete dwellings of part of the new Reykjavik, built round a small lake and against a backdrop of bare mountains.

28–30 *Opposite:* An early example of Scandinavian craftsmanship – the graceful decorated prow of the ninth-century Norwegian Oseberg ship. *Right:* 'Divers', metal sculpture by the contemporary Finnish woman sculptor, Eila Hiltunen, whose mastery of movement is remarkable. *Below:* Group of 'Angels', by the Swede Carl Milles, also noted for his sense of fluidity and movement.

31 Some examples of modern Scandinavian design. *Above:* Goblet in roughly moulded glass by Timo Sarpaneva (Finland). *Above, right:* Pewter cocktail set by John Gulbrandsrød (Norway). *Right:* Chamotte vase by Annikki Hovisaari (Finland), and below it, bold silver rings by Jan Lundgren (Sweden). *Below:* Simple table silver by Annelise Bjørner and Rigmor Andersen of Georg Jensen (Denmark).

8 Norway

NORWAY (*Norge* to the Norwegians) is in many respects the most personable of the Nordic countries. This is partly because of the heroic mould in which it is cast. Its landscapes have the same striking juxtaposition of forms as those of Switzerland. Indeed, Honoré de Balzac referred to Norway as Switzerland by the sea. In contrast to the gentle, almost feminine graces of the Danish countryside, Norway is muscular and masculine. At the same time because of its wealth of legend and lore, the name of Norway is one of the earliest to enter the schoolroom. Maelström and midnight sun, lemming and Lapp, Odin and Thor filter into consciousness at an early age. Moreover, Norway is familiar through the communications of six generations of tourists, who by comparison with those who went to other lands seem to have left a disproportionately large literary legacy. Fishermen and hunters, climbers and skiers, yachtsmen and artists all committed their experiences to paper. The guidebooks of Murray, Baedeker and Cook went through successive editions. They make splendidly nostalgic reading from the days when Norway was really *à la mode* – when the crowned heads of Europe turned north and the Kaiser Wilhelm sought Valhalla in the Sognefjord.

The personality of Norway that they glimpsed is elusive as is that of all countries. It can be tracked down partly in its strong spirit of place. This is inseparable from the juxtaposition of highland and lowland, the interplay of mountain and water. The grouping of mountains is infinitely varied along more than a thousand miles of coast. The salt water, tugged strongly by tides, from which they often rise precipitately, exaggerates their height; while the lakes in the dales multiply them by reflection. But for the most part in Norway, as the landscape is tumultuous, so the seascape is turbulent. The seas that shape its coastal platforms, multiplying archipelagos and devouring islands, are stormy. High above them ice still grinds inexorably, scaling down mountain and plateau, gouging out valleys; while, when they escape from their winter refrigeration, the quick succession of freeze and thaw shatters the resistance of the peaks.

And all these features are subject to what is, for most parts of the world, an unusual interplay of light and darkness. Norway's seasonal rhythm is common to all of Scandinavia, but in most of Norway its effects are exaggerated by the lie of the land. As in the Alps, fjord and dale have their sunny and shady sides. A high incidence of cloud also modifies luminosity over most of Norway. Cloud may add poetry to the landscape, but it brings problems to the land. Two other features may be recorded. Firstly, because of Norway's great length, the seasons may also be followed for weeks on end. The magic of spring can be pursued latitudinally until in Troms and Finnmark it merges floristically with summer. Tulip, lupin, peony, monkshood, giant hogweed all bloom together. Secondly, altitude offers ubiquitous floral contrasts. The Arctic prevails on the fells (indeed, for the purposes of the cinema, Captain Scott's Antarctic), while at their feet a *côte fleurie* rivals with its froth of apple and cherry blossom the higher snows.

Mountain and water, sunshine and shadow are common features, yet the general impression of Norway is one of immense versatility. Each fjord and valley differs from the neighbours in the unappreciated but critical chemistry of its rocks (and therefore in the way that they erode), in the local characteristics of its climate, in the legacy contributed by its past inhabitants.

In these varying landscapes is distilled the life of Norway – the amalgam of the lives of Norwegians. All show a highly particularized expression of place – the vernacular architecture, the detail of farm implements, the design of folk costume, the character of dialects. Nationally this produces a paradox. On the one hand, the physical unit of each valley or fjord has fostered a distinct local community. Formerly each was sufficient unto itself; contemporarily each retains its independent outlook. On the other hand, the claustrophobic atmosphere of the fjord made for what a nineteenth-century novelist called a half-monastic existence where men turned in upon themselves to become a race apart; and where frequent insufficiencies and poverty yielded the bitter wrath of the novelist Knut Hamsun.

It is difficult to imagine how national unity could be created out of this scattered congeries of highly particularized communities. Yet there are unifying forces. There is, for example, the common experience of living dangerously. Norway is a land of natural hazards – storm and blizzard, avalanche and rock fall. Norwegians have been described as living in armed neutrality with nature. In some this breeds a sense of despair, but more often it arouses a sense of adventure. Although science has helped to reduce the physical hazards for those who work closely with nature, a cultivated and sustained physical and mental discipline is still widely demanded of Norwegians. This is no less for those who engage in the art of adventure vicariously. Climbing, ski-ing, sailing, hiking are the relaxations of townsfolk – all of whom are physically near enough to untamed land and sea to enjoy their pleasures but to appreciate their challenges. Nor can intuition fail to be essential for people who must make their own interpretations of signs in the sky, on the water or on the mountain.

A second unifying force is the carefully collected and disseminated folk heritage. In Norway community of feeling owes much to music and folklore. This sentiment has been strengthened by composers who have given new romantic overtones to the traditional songs first collected by Magnus Landstad. Edvard Grieg has been for Norway what Frederic Chopin has been for Poland. Norway even has a national anthem which can be sung without embarrassment. Folk music is inseparable from the dance, traditional forms of which are learnt in the schoolroom throughout Norway. For accompaniment the adopted instruments of seamen – concertina and harmonica – are likely to take precedence over the nine-stringed Hardanger fiddle. The heritage of song and dance come into their own on festive occasions, public or private. The bonfires of Johannes (Midsummer Eve) or of St Olav's (Olsok or Olav's wake, as it is popularly called) are fitting backgrounds for the ring dance; while the sober orations of Constitution Day on 17 May are accompanied by a climax of music and flag-waving unparalleled in all Scandinavia. Artists, their works reproduced in engravings, have given visual support – Adolf Tidemand, J. F. Eckersberg and J. C. C. Dahl.

An element of piquancy is conveyed to the personality of Norway by a supernatural streak passed on by generations of imaginative story-tellers. No Scandinavian country has generated a greater number of folk stories and their *dramatis personae* are unique to Norway. Trolls, exploding when the sun shines on them, retreat to mountain halls more commodious than anything conceived in Irish fantasies. *Huldre* – women tailed if not hoofed beneath their bedraggled skirts – haunt the upland pastures. *Draug* – or water sprites – occupy the waterfalls; while Lapland's witches and 'sellers of wind' have occupied their own particular niche in European literature for generations. These supernatural beings have contributed an abundance of place-names, at large and in detail. Trolltinden, Trollstiga and Jotunheim are names whose fame has spread beyond their homeland. A seeming corpus of fact has developed around the monsters and serpents that inhabit the surrounding seas. William Guthrie (1786) rejoiced in 'the mermen and mer-women . . . resident in Norwegian Seas'. Erik Pontoppidan's weighty *Natural History* (1752–53) took sea serpents as a matter of course, while in J. H. Tuckey's respectable *Maritime Geography* (1815) the Kraken itself awoke. Within living memory there is testimony from reliable witnesses as convincing as that for any unidentified flying objects. Hallucination, bred of dietary deficiencies as well as of alcoholic excesses, may explain some of the revelations, for perceptual projection is easy amid rock fantasies, twisted vegetation and swirling mists. And artists have conspired to invest these features with half-human shapes. Thomas Kittelsen and Erik Werenskiöld created galleries of fantasticks as real as most portraits of historical personages. Fabulous is an adjective which cannot be misapplied to Norway.

Between the teeming but invisible life of the surrounding seas and the haunting, even haunted, solitudes of the fells are concentrated Norway's nearly four million people. About a third of them live around Oslofjord, with the capital central to a semi-circle of sizeable towns which stretch from Sarpsborg in the south-east to Drammen in the south-west. Another half million people are gathered together on the slopes of the seven hills up which Hanseatic Bergen climbs, on the lowland promontories that focus upon St Swithun's Cathedral in bustling Stavanger, and on the fertile sweep of Trondheimfjord, where the archiepiscopal seat of old Nidaros (Trondheim) is at the fulcrum of the country. Yet in spite of these concentrations, it is rare to be out of sight of habitation either along the extended coast or over much of the interior.

There are several reasons why unpopulated Norway appears to be so populous. Firstly, the cities apart, settlement is dispersed rather than concentrated. Secondly, most houses stand out from their báckground rather than retreating into it, since wood and stucco are usually colour-washed. Thirdly, most settlement is along the old-established routes that visitors to Norway follow. The coastal route, identified as the Inner Lead on maritime charts, has been followed since prehistoric times. Inland, the network of communications is less finely drawn than in many European countries so that the great majority of homes are visible from the highways.

Most roads and railways are feats of engineering. The Bergen–Oslo railway (one of Europe's most scenic routes), the Flåm railway (cork-screwing down 3,000 feet from the western plateau to Aurlandsfjord in Sogne), the Ofoten railway (pitched steeply from the Kiruna ore-fields to Narvik), Nordlandsbanen (built by wartime conscript labour), the Sørland railway (playing hide-and-seek through dozens of tunnels) – each has a highly distinctive history. The automobile has demanded a transformation of roads. Yet though the land is more compliant to modern road-building machinery, a residue of fearfulness remains along most highways. It is encountered for example in the yawning chasm above Rjukanfoss, in the frowning rock face out of which is blasted the road to the head of Sörfjord, and in the multiple hairpins that have enabled the engineer to conduct traffic from Sognefjord over Sognefjell. Cables also bind Norway together – heavy copper having yielded to lighter aluminium and alloy. Sometimes, as across Sognefjord, they may swing several miles between their supports. The electricity and telephone lines that stride across the wilderness, scale the heights and slip through the shallows of the surrounding archipelagos present major problems of construction and maintenance. So, too, at a lowlier level do the farmers' telfer lines that are indispensable for transporting hay and milk from the inaccessible uplands to lower-level road or waterway. Television antennae and transmission masts try to overcome the problem of beaming programmes to all the nooks and crannies of this much-dissected land. The same applies to the radar beams vital for domestic aircraft.

Internal transport routes formerly played a more limited role in Norway, since most movement was by sea. The sea remains the most recurrent theme in Norwegian life. Norway is committed to it, dependent on it – indeed, as Ibsen declared, hypnotized by it. From the daily weather forecasts the nation is as familiar with the multitude of names used for its invisible banks as it is with the heights and plateaux of the land. In a variety of ways the sea has compensated for the deficiencies of the land. Food from the sea has always been available in quantities far beyond domestic needs. From earliest times it has therefore offered goods for export – their range, variety and markets multiplying prodigiously through canning, refrigeration and processing. The sea has provided food for animals as well as for men. Wind-dried herring are still fed to cattle along the coast, though deodorized fish meal is more in keeping with the modern idiom. Mink farmers also look to herring. In its own right the sea provides nourishment for the land. Seaweed is a valuable manure for the many diminutive fields of coastal Norway, while the processed offal from fish factories has an old-established place as a fertilizer. In prehistoric times the sea also provided winter clothing. Today the harvest of the sealer is culled for the more exclusive sector of the apparel industry and the pelt of the polar bear is a luxury product. Even light and heat have come from the sea, though the whales whose blubber supplied them have suffered grievously from over-exploitation. The same fate has overtaken the whaling enterprise in the Antarctic that Norwegians pioneered.

With the development of large-scale overseas trading, it was easy for the Norwegians to capitalize on their sea-going experience. No country specializes more fundamentally in the carrying trade than Norway. Fully 40,000 people are engaged directly in the operation of one of the world's three largest and most up-to-date mercantile marines. The 20 million tons of shipping, operated primarily by a shipping aristocracy which stands apart in this egalitarian society, is equally divided between tankers and other specialist vessels. At the same time, the community of master shipwrights whose ancestors established the shipbuilding tradition have adapted their skills to new methods of construction. Once more, Norwegian shipyards look to domestically produced materials, with ships' plate and steel components from Mo i Rana as modern equivalent of the timbers formerly felled in the coastal woodlands. Oslo no longer retains the monopoly of large-scale yards. Stavanger has the capacity to launch from its slipways the world's largest gas tankers (of 100,000 tons dead weight); while the hulls of vessels of equal if not greater tonnage also tower above the waterfronts of Haugesund and Bergen.

Not all of the old skills are directed into these new giants of the seas. Carpenters and designers still design custom-built vessels. In modest workshops such as those in Flekkefjord a year of loving care by a team of craftsmen may be devoted to a racing yacht, though it is more likely to be for the princely purse of a foreign buyer than for the home market. Smaller pleasure boats are for everybody today. And while smaller fishing vessels continue to be constructed to both old-established and new designs, at the other end of the scale Norwegian enterprise has resulted in the delivery of the world's largest fish-factory ship for use in Arctic waters. With the decline of whale hunting, units of the Antarctic fishing fleet are also ripe for conversion to such new uses.

Adjustments in the maritime relationship have parallels on the land, where traditional practices still linger beside new methods. The Westland, for all its abundant vegetation and bright summer flowers, is not kind to farmers. It yields rich natural grass for summer grazing, but it is often better to ensile than to make hay of the sown grasses intended for winter fodder. The long hayracks may be picturesque, but they are a reflection of the high frequency of rainfall and proclaim a low-nutrient crop. Potatoes may thrive and oats may be harvested; but save for the apple and cherry orchards that line the fjord edge of Hardanger and to a lesser extent Sognefjord, and for limited animal husbandry, the centre of gravity of farming is in east Norway. Here is the breadbasket of the country; though even the seemingly extensive wheat and barley fields of the dry sunny and sheltered eastern valleys and dales are inadequate to meet domestic needs. The retreat from the historic upland pastures continues, while the value of the more accessible forest pastures in the east is higher for timber than for grazing. Yet relics of transhumance remain – cattle and goats struggle up and down rocky paths to the lush high-level pastures and the handful of grey wooden hutments, where relics of an earlier dairying culture linger. The forest strengthens farming in east Norway. The rising value of softwoods, the more economic methods of handling them, the spread of scientific management have all resulted in a re-appraisal of the timber lot. Although Norway lacks the extensive woodlands of Sweden or Finland, it has common standards of production and research. In the forest at least, Norway is able to reaffirm the values of rural life.

Mining has also made a more limited impact upon Norway than upon Sweden. It results in two highly contrasted landscapes. The deserted mines and relict settlements of former times are illustrated by

Kongsberg and Röros. Kongsberg silver mines, now no more than a tourist attraction, supported a formerly wealthy community which built a church like a cathedral and handsome patrician houses. Although Röros has become a winter sports centre, it is also rich in external evidence from its mining past. The spoil heaps and miners' cabins, the deserted smelteries and workshops recall a copper town, the decline of which was captured for posterity in Johan Falkberget's novel *Christianus Sextus*.

In direct contrast to these echoes from the past are the modern mining and mineral-working sites. It is equally fair to regard them as blemishes on the local landscape, and as signs of wealth in a frequently impoverished countryside. The low-grade iron ore of Syd Varanger, partially refined as taconite before export, has given new life to the eastern extremities of Finnmark province. The low-grade coal of inhospitable Spitsbergen keeps several thousand men busy extracting half a million tons annually for consumption in north Norway. In Nordland province, copper production at Sulitjelma has been sustained and Dunderland iron ores have been revalued. The identification of rare minerals such as uranium, titanium, niobium and thorium has set in train a new age of prospecting and, in the process, has called for a more precise definition of property boundaries in the superficially barren fells. The new-found wealth is largely electrically processed against the background of two generations of experience in aluminium smelteries at such centres as Höyanger, Årdal and Sunndalsöra. The manufacture of ferrous and non-ferrous alloys makes equal demands upon electricity; while the state-sponsored iron and steel complex at Mo i Rana also looks to water power as the basic source of energy. Electro-chemical industries have been added to electro-metallurgical. Norway already made a European impact before the First World War with the Norsk Hydro nitrate plant. The military implications of the associated heavy-water plant at Rjukan are remembered from commando raids during the Second World War. Chemicals have greatly diversified Norwegian industry.

The development of these new industries, the growth of the communicational network and the rapidly rising standard of living have created a great demand for energy. Thanks to rugged relief and high precipitation. Norway has one of Europe's richest concentrations of water power. Formerly the scale of operations needed to harness it was often so large that exploitation was retarded; but now financial resources rather than technical fact rs are serious restraints. In particular, new methods of removing rock have eased excavation. Warrens of tunnels which gather together waters from a number of natural high-level reservoirs are features of such a system as that at Tokke. While the scenic amenities of such renowned falls as Rjukanfoss may have been lost to posterity, the natural harmony of the landscape is increasingly preserved by the construction of underground conduits and power plants. Energy supplies are unevenly distributed in Norway; nor do peak load and peak supply coincide. The resources of the north, where altitudes are lower and rainfall less, are smaller than those of the west. Run-off is lowest in winter when need is largest. Exceptionally dry summers may also cause difficulties. Demand is absolutely greatest around Oslofjord, but long-distance transmission has reduced problems of supply. Finally, oil and atomic energy may both compete with or supplement hydro-electric power, while the prospects of oil and natural gas from North Sea concessions are good.

The unevenness of economic development in Norway, resulting from the country's shape, has been exaggerated in the twentieth century. The problems of the north country are common to Sweden and Finland, but the details differ in Norway. In general the northern third of Norway is less accessible to the rest of the country, resources are less evenly distributed and population is more concentrated along the coast than in north Sweden and Finland.

Population is more mixed ethnographically than in any other part of the country. There has been Norwegian intermarriage with both immigrant Finns and native Lapps. Names on the land as well as local dialects also reflect this mixture. Population is more mobile than in other parts of Norway. The movement from country to town is not without its positive features – for example, it facilitates the provision of social services. Population outflow is a different matter, partly because the generous movement to the south is mostly of younger people. In so far as it is isolated and neglected, it is natural that north Norway should be radical in its thinking. Norway's old-established socialist government has attempted to ease the lot of the underdeveloped northlands. Furthermore, the planned reconstruction of Finnmark and Troms following wartime destruction has been succeeded by planned development. The programme of assistance includes financial support and sponsorship of industrial and workshop enterprises, price supports for farm produce, transport subsidies, and educational investment – not least in the emerging Tromsö university. Supplementary benefits are written into the salaries of civil servants who work in the north, though social conscience and patriotic duty both stir some to undertake a period of northern service. Nevertheless, the attitudes of northerners are all too little understood by those who inhabit the deep south, most of whom have not set foot in the high north.

Despite shortcomings and hardships, it is difficult to deny a sense of exhilaration in places such as Tromsö and Hammerfest, which have been and remain the points of departure for expeditions and enterprises to the Arctic. Memorials in public places to national figures such as Roald Amundsen and international explorers such as Umberto Nobile have their counterparts in headstones which bear the titles 'Arctic Ocean Trader' and 'Arctic Ocean Captain'. Such merchants and skippers have also been aware that international rivalries afflict the icy wastes to which their homeland is the threshold. Svalbard (Spitsbergen) continues to yield its relics – from weapons and tools to the scorbutic skeletons that recall the great days of whaling. North Norway has a scatter of military cemeteries where Russian, Pole, Frenchman, German and Englishman lie side by side. In north Norway NATO marches beside the Warsaw Pact, and though the front line of the Pasvik river is tranquillity itself, the shifting military population of the garrison territory of Finnmark and Troms adds to the inherent restlessness of a community on the outposts of European settlement.

Political life in Norway generally follows an undramatic course. The Storting, or parliament, is unicameral, with 150 members. Although the Labour Party usually dominates the Storting, it has not always had an absolute majority, and there have been periods of coalition. The other parties, which individually command significantly less support than Labour, are: Conservative, Liberal, Centre (formerly Agrarian), Christian People's, Socialist People's, and Communist – the last being one of the weakest of its persuasion in Scandinavia. In 1971 an all-Labour government took over from the previous coalition, although two votes short of an absolute majority. However, the other parties in the two preceding coalitions had had disagreements, and conditions pointed to a more decisive style of government than had been pursued for a time.

Norwegian stresses are more evident socially – even geographically – than they are in narrowly political spheres. It is easy to find paradoxes in any country – paradoxes which ultimately resolve themselves. Three are abiding in Norway. Firstly, the stresses arising from the two varieties of the language still echo in the schoolroom. The anti-Danish supporters of the romantic poet Henrik Wergeland and of the grammarian Ivar Aasen still pit their country tongue against the literary language so vigorously defended by Björnstjerne Björnson. And because of the succession of spelling reforms that has accompanied the schism, it is facetiously remarked that a woman's age can be told from the way she spells. Yet, despite language differences reminiscent of those encountered by Lemuel Gulliver in his travels, Norway is charged with national feeling. As with Finland, this sentiment has been strengthened by threats of national extinction during the Second World War. The challenge from without to a young independent state lies behind much of Norway's thought and action. The challenge is exaggerated by Norway's limited population – and perhaps the great friezes of life represented in the vast murals at Oslo Town Hall or the Vigeland park with its crowded sculptures are expressions of a subconscious wish to correct the deficiency.

Secondly and not unrelated to the first paradox, there is behind a relaxed, often opportunist, exterior, a strong interior discipline and principle. *Peer Gynt* has his reverse in *Brand*. The brilliant nightmares of expressionism conceived by Edvard Munch, a Norwegian artist of world stature, are matched by sober photographs of the master builders of modern Norway, who keep watch in school room and board room. In the personality of Norway is bound up a continuing respect for those who have shaped its independent fortunes.

Finally, despite the technical, economic and social metamorphosis of their land, Norwegians still pulse strongly to the rhythms of nature. This reaction is inseparable from the swing of the seasons and the commitment to the sea. The surge of the Lofoten cod in February and March or of the herring off Ålesund in April move entire communities as they did in the days when the first Norwegian traders brought knowledge of them to the court of King Alfred.

9   Sweden

SWEDEN (*Sverige* to the Swedes) is the victim, in an international context, of the preconceived superlative. Clichés, true and false, but too often couched in superlatives, have been absorbed by those who have never set foot in Scandinavia: Sweden is the most prosperous country in Europe (true, though the bogeys of inflation and balance of payments often come too close for comfort); wages are relatively higher than in any other country (true); there are more telephones per head of the population than in any other country (true); there are more suicides than in any other country (false); there are more divorces than anywhere else (false); alcoholism is more widespread than anywhere else (take with a pinch of salt and a spoonful of interpretation).

There are many other superlatives, which, right or wrong, have not been earned without some basis in fact. Since the end of the First World War Sweden has been moving with only occasional setbacks up the ladder towards a high material prosperity and a high welfare society. The transition from an agricultural to an industrial country has gone forward steadily and generally smoothly, and the Swedes, with Switzerland as their model, have built their industrial success on quality. Observance of their neutrality brought them out of the Second World War with a long lead over the rest of Europe – a lead which they quite deliberately exploited, while giving generous help to less fortunate countries, Finland in particular. So, since 1945, the economy has been able to expand at a considerably greater rate in Sweden than elsewhere in Europe – and to expand as a result of long-term policies well thought out in advance. It has been said, though not authenticated, that when, in the Second World War, the Swedes realized that Germany would be beaten and that the German orbit in which they had previously lived would disintegrate, they immediately began to discuss policies which would enable them to stand on their own feet in the post-war world. One of their main supports was to be education, and their plans for a highly educated population were gestated for so long that it was only in 1962 that they began to be put fully into practice. From 1945, too, dates a linguistic reorientation highly impressive to British and American visitors: a cult of the English language so powerful that, in Stockholm at least, one begins to feel that English is not so much a foreign tongue as the common second language of the country.

Industrialization and urbanization have inevitably gone hand in hand, although it is not uncommon to find industrial plants in the countryside. In 1920 55 per cent of the population lived in villages; by 1960 this figure had dropped to 27 per cent. The size of the country (173,665 square miles) means that, outside the cities, there are vast tracts of uninhabited land, whether in the plains of the south, or, to a far greater extent, in the forest areas stretching northwards from Gästrikland to Norrbotten, and known collectively as Norrland (the North Land).

The length of the country (980 miles from top to toe) gives it a great variety of landscape, ranging from the modest glaciers of the north to the sandy beaches of the south-west, from the great lakes of the centre to the numberless islands of the coastal archipelagos. The mountains of Norrland, rising to several thousand feet, and enclosing deep valleys cut through by great rivers, lakes and rapids, share something of Norway's scenic magnificence, although they cannot rival the splendour of the western fjord country. The northern half of Sweden inclines to the south-east, and the rivers which drain down from the mountains into the Gulf of Bothnia have provided the principal source of the country's electric power; and although the presence of industry is evident in what was once a near-wilderness, the Swedes of the last three decades have made considerable efforts in landscaping and re-afforestation, so that despoiling has been minimized. And in more recent years Sweden has moved ahead of most of Europe in an energetic attack on pollution, including a law controlling industrial effluent. This, however, was not before several of its finest lakes had reached the stage at which neither fish could live nor man swim.

As in Finland, much of the landscape takes its character from woodland and water, yet the proportions and the mixture differ. There is nothing in Sweden which resembles the great labyrinthine lake system of eastern Finland, where in some parishes water occupies a greater area than land. Finland, however, has no lakes containing as much water as Vänern, Vättern and Mälaren, which together with the smaller Hjälmaren straddle the country from west to east. The forests, principally pine, spruce and birch, cover just over half the total land area, while in Finland they occupy nearly three-quarters.

Especially in the more populated south the countryside has a certain neatness of aspect, lent in particular by the uniformity and chequerboard planning of so many villages and small towns. The kings of seventeenth- and eighteenth-century Sweden were interested town planners, and introduced, partly to reduce fire hazards, the chequerboard into their realms even before it achieved greater fame and development in the USA. This addiction to a chilly regularity has persisted into modern times. Stockholm, for instance, has lakeside garden suburbs, built mainly in the 1920s, of enviable beauty. But its post-war overspill has been housed in somewhat inhuman suburban towns where functionalism fights the living green. One of the best-known and earliest of these developments is Vällingby, which, it used to be alleged, produced the highest suicide rate in the land. Whether true or not, it can certainly be said that there is little in Vällingby and similar places to lift up the hearts of those who live in them. Yet today Vällingby is considered almost idyllic by comparison with Skärholmen's unrelieved acres of concrete. Examples of advanced planning these towns certainly are – Farsta, for instance, gets its district heating from a nuclear power plant – but the advance often seems to be in the direction of a type of super-institutionalized existence.

A slight technical melancholy is beginning to creep into Stockholm itself. Here, not long ago, was one of Europe's most attractive cities, built almost on water, and yielding recurrent vistas of tree-fringed lake, islands, and the arm of the sea which stretches as it narrows right into the city centre. The historical core of Stockholm is an island known as Gamla Stan, the Old Town, whose ancient buildings flank narrow streets, and include the Royal Palace, the Cathedral and the Stock Exchange. Formerly, though the Old Town was unmistakeably medieval, the buildings in the larger city which grew up around it were of such varying periods and styles as to give a sense of historical continuity and gradual development. Many of the more important buildings of the past remain, but in the sixties large tracts of the town were rebuilt in a modern idiom, according well with the intellectual attitude of contemporary Swedes, while leaving many of them less at home than in the past. Even when one puts aside the question whether these tower blocks which use such quantities of glass are suitable for a northern climate, the visual reconciliation of ancient and modern remains difficult, and often suggests that for the architects and town planners of today the past is dead, and preferably forgotten. Hence a certain nostalgia among older citizens; and, less to be expected, growing protest from the young.

But water, trees and green spaces still make Stockholm a pleasant place, especially in summer. Areas of parkland remain close to its centre, notably the delightful Skansen. Here is the world's first and still largest open-air museum, to which have been transplanted from various parts of Sweden ancient dwellings, farm buildings, workshops, mills and a church. Combined with restaurants, entertainments, arenas and a zoo, they make Skansen an outstanding example of the way pleasure, interest and relaxation can be provided relatively cheaply for all ages and types of people.

Stockholm's greatest asset, however, is the archipelago which begins on the fringe of the city, and continues, with its hundreds of islands and its thousands of creeks and bays, for miles before it loses itself in the Baltic. Here is 'Summer Stockholm', a land of escape dotted with cottages made warmly red by the Falun copper paint which protects them, and bound together by a network of steamer routes, yachts, motor boats, and, inevitably, oil storage depots.

Gothenburg (Göteborg) is Sweden's largest seaport and second largest town, whose west coast situation conveys an extrovert Atlantic feeling contrasting with the introvert atmosphere of Baltic Stockholm. In the seventeenth century, along with foreigners of many other nationalities, Dutchmen settled in Gothenburg, and their strong influence upon the centre of the city is seen in its canals. This windswept, lively city has its own clearly defined personality, a part of which is a healthy self-regard and a corresponding scorn of Stockholm. Turku looks likewise at Helsinki, Bergen at Oslo, and Glasgow even more so at Edinburgh. It gains its self-confidence from the va-et-vient of international trade, the principal reason for its existence. Its industrial prosperity derives primarily from shipbuilding, although it has not managed to escape the crises known to shipbuilders elsewhere in Europe. But it does not suffer from the single-industry sickness of some shipbuilding towns. Both Volvo and SKF, one of the world's great producers of ball- and roller-bearings, have important plants in Gothenburg, and the Göta River valley behind it is lined with a great variety of factories. Now, with a port entrance deepened to take larger tankers, and new quays looking for container traffic, Gothenburg believes that it may eventually become the central port for the whole of Scandinavia.

In a country as elongated and as relatively thinly populated as Sweden centrifugal forces are strong. A tradition of centralization is counteracted by persistent regional feelings. Malmö, facing Copenhagen across the Sound, is the natural regional capital of the south. Formerly it was dominated by nearby Lund. Today, with their roles reversed, Lund is a university and cathedral town, and Malmö one of the fastest-growing cities in Sweden. As a port and traffic junction, and as the focus of a group of smaller towns, it is central to the Swedish half of the Öresund conurbation. Already economics echo the historical situation in which Malmö and its province of Skåne belonged not to Sweden, but to Denmark.

Stockholm, Gothenburg and Malmö have the largest industrial concentrations in the country. However, Sweden, like the other Scandinavian countries, has escaped most of the ugly urban development which the industrial revolution brought to Western Europe and north-eastern USA. Industry in Sweden is widely scattered, often near sources of raw materials and water power, and often relatively small as to the number of employees in any single plant. The rivers flowing into the Gulf of Bothnia provide estuarine sites for ports and wood-processing centres from Haparanda in the north, through Luleå and Umeå to Gävle in central Sweden. The engineering industry, developing later and related to the metallurgy of the Bergslagen area, took shape along the great lakes axis, at places such as Västerås, Motala, Eskilstuna and Husqvarna. Sweden is, and always has been, the most highly industrialized of the Scandinavian countries. Stora Kopparberg, the company which owns both Scandinavia's largest steel works and Europe's second largest paper mill, was founded in the twelfth century, and now claims to be the oldest chartered company still in existence in the world. An American survey in 1970 of the two hundred largest industrial enterprises outside the United States included six Swedish firms, but none from any other Scandinavian country. These six were typical of the orientation of Swedish industry, being concerned with manufacture of metal products, automobiles, tractors, ball bearings, electronic and telecommunications equipment. Sweden has sometimes been called a land of poets and engineers, but the engineers have invariably made the greater impact on the outside world.

The development of the engineering industry is favoured by raw material resources. From the seventeenth to the nineteenth century Sweden was a producer of pig iron for the world. Today the Lapland iron deposits are among the largest high-grade ores in the world, and the greater part of their production is exported. In Västerbotten a metallurgical complex centred on Boliden produces copper, lead and iron pyrites on a considerable scale. Sweden's second great natural resource lies in its forests, whose processed products, in the form of chemical and mechanical pulp, paper and wallboard, command world markets. The third important resource is water power, which compensates for the near-absence of coal or oil. The Swedes have done much to perfect long-distance transmission of electricity, so that their integrated grid enables the areas of surplus energy in the north to be linked with areas of deficiency in the south. The Ume and Lule river systems have been developed with transatlantic speed and efficiency; and there are now in hand considerable plans to generate nuclear power. Given these three rich and complementary resources, it can easily be seen why Sweden has had so long a lead over the rest of Scandinavia, and a lead accentuated by neutrality in two world wars.

A good deal of thinking before the Second World War credited Sweden with having found a middle way between capitalism and socialism. The Swedes were never particularly contentious about certain areas of nationalization and had, for instance, taken it for granted from the start that their excellent railway system should be publicly owned. But while in postwar decades other countries have acrimoniously made their way towards more extensive nationalization, the state in Sweden today has a less direct hand in industry than France, Italy or Great Britain. In spite of a firm tendency to increase government intervention, Sweden remains a country in which private enterprise has thrived alongside a Social-Democratic party which has been in power, with only minor interruptions, since 1932. On the other hand, there also thrives a co-operative movement of larger relative dimensions than can be found in most other European countries. It is Sweden's largest trading enterprise, still constantly expanding and increasing its share of the total market. Its size and influence derive principally from its triple role of manufacturer, wholesaler and retailer. Its manufacturing side, launched originally as part of a cartel-cracking operation, now produces paper and pulp, cash registers, building materials and ceramics, food, textiles and household goods. Its shops include not only the smaller local branches but numerous department stores and supermarkets. Other areas in which co-operatives play an important part are housing, petrol and service stations, insurance and agriculture.

In domestic policy, the Social-Democratic party has tended to keep out of industry and to concentrate on social benefits, education (see Chapter 10) and the environment. Its prevailing philosophy has been egalitarian, and, if the claims of equality and liberty were to come into conflict, liberty might be the loser. Almost as important has been its insistence on the right of the individual to pensions and benefits provided by the state. The Swedes being naturally a hard-working people, the government has had little need to balance rights and responsibilities; but there are spheres in which the individual's only right is to do exactly what the government, central or local, tells him to do. He has, for instance, virtually no choice as to which school he will send his children to. By and large, the individual, for good or ill, according to his point of view, feels the influence of government to a greater extent than business and other organized groups.

Probably the area of economic life best known in the outside world is labour relations. Sweden has presented a near-idyllic picture of a country without strikes, in which all industrial difficulties appeared to be settled in an atmosphere of sweet reasonableness. Until the late sixties this picture was only slightly exaggerated. There were strikes but only on a small scale. The individual worker and employer accepted their mutual contractual relationships. The longstanding and permanent machinery for the regulation of management-labour relations – a committee with seven representatives from each side – seemed to function well, partly stimulated by the desire to avoid government intervention felt by both sides, as well as by the government itself. Ninety per cent of workers were unionized and welded into the single LO (Confederation of Trades Unions), union membership was voluntary, and the closed shop was not generally practised. (There was a union, of a sort, for those who did not believe in unions!)

An important factor has been that Swedish workers have understood better than most of their European colleagues that good social security and welfare can be bought only by a thriving economy, and in that respect have been willing to reconcile socialism and profit. But, concurrently with a formidable wages-prices explosion, an attack of living beyond one's means and a counter-attack of swingeing taxation, a series of wild-cat strikes broke out in 1969. A particular shock to the Swedes was that one of the longest took place at the nationalized Kiruna ironworks in Lapland. Among the workers' main complaints was the fact that union officials were out of touch and far away – an unfortunate symptom of a society reaching the size and complexity where communications become less effective, and may even break down. (At the same time, individual members of the co-operative movement were complaining that they could no longer make their voices heard.) The relative harmony induced by life in a small country where so many people know each other, and where, more important still, so many people think along the same lines, was clearly diminishing. Sweden thus came into the seventies facing for the first time the more serious problems of communication that beset Europe's larger countries.

The early seventies brought a strike of civil servants (including judges, teachers and railway administrators), symptomatic of a change less expected than that of weakening communications. This was a weakening belief, among the middle-aged at least, in the hither-to almost sacred principle of equality; or, more specifically, dis-illusionment with its practical application. The civil servants went on strike principally because their own living standards were gradually being whittled away by increases in industrial wages partly aimed at bringing white- and blue-collar earnings into some sort of parity. Already some more highly paid industrial workers were protesting against settlements which reduced their differentials. But if equality was beginning to lose its appeal for older Swedes, it compensated by increasing its hold on the younger generation, and this sharpening of divisions by age group indicated yet another change in attitudes.

In the wider context of national life also, there was an air of general change against a relatively stable background. The elderly monarch, King Gustaf VI Adolf, born in 1882, was respected everywhere for his ability and unpretentiousness. Yet among younger Swedes there was a considerable movement in favour of a republic and among the older generation a growing feeling that the monarchy would eventually be brought to an end, though perhaps not in its time. Meanwhile the king continues the traditional practice of presiding over weekly cabinet meetings, though as a neutral and non-political figure.

The constitution, too, was set for change. For a century Sweden had had a bicameral system, but in 1971, with the agreement of all parties, the Upper House was abolished. The new single chamber was enlarged, and elected for a period of three years, instead of four as previously. Of the 350 members of the new Parliament (or, in Swedish, *riksdag*), 310 are elected by proportional representation in the 28 constituencies; the remaining 40 seats are divided between the parties in such a way that almost complete proportionality can be achieved. An interesting sidelight on the workings of proportional representation in Sweden is that it has maintained the Social Democratic party in power since 1932, and has brought about only minor shifts in relative party strength. In other countries, for example Finland, proportional representation has been held responsible for the fragmentation of parties and instability of governments. In the past certain technical electoral arrangements have accentuated the no-change tendency, but they have not been wholly responsible for it. If reasons can be found, they are more likely to lie in the hitherto non-argumentative character of the Swedes, and their general unwillingness to be involved in complicated issues. They have created a tolerant society, but it is difficult to estimate how much of their tolerance is active, how much passive. Passivity is certainly suggested by the acquiescence of the individual (perhaps now past its peak) in bureaucratic regulation of his life, in interference and sometimes plain nosey-parkering, as in some of the highly private and personal questions included in census forms.

Nevertheless, party political life persists, and it may be regarded as an achievement for any party to remain in opposition and in relatively good shape for forty or so years, as in Sweden. The opposition parties have not only persisted, but, like the Social Democrats, have maintained their strength, more or less, over the years. Up to 1970 the Social Democrats held between 40 and 50 per cent of all votes, the rest being divided between the other parties in the following descending order: Centre Party (formerly Agrarian), Liberal, Conservative, Communist. The 1970 election showed slight movements to left and right, and allowed the Social Democrats to retain power only with the support of the Communists. They have had this experience before, though the relatively moderate Communist Party has not exerted any appreciable influence on policy.

But the sixties had already seen two new developments in political life. The more surprising of the two was the provision of state subsidies for all parties, proportionate to seats held and votes cast. In spite of strong opposition, the Social Democrats held to the view that the smaller parties would otherwise disintegrate for lack of funds, and that they must be subsidized in order to continue the job of political education necessary for the maintenance of an informed opposition.

While the real danger of a static political situation was officially recognized, signs of a natural reaction also began to be seen. In the 1964 general election a new party, the Christian Democratic Union, appeared on the scene. While it failed to get any members into Parliament, it had more success in local politics. Another sign that a section at least of the public was beginning to equate stability with stagnation was the formation of an organization called the Citizens' Front. Its principal aim was to rally and, if possible, associate the opposition parties, in the hope of dislodging the Social Democrats from their entrenched governmental position.

Since 1809, however, Sweden has had its own individual embodiment of governmental checks and balances in the ombudsman. His function has always been to investigate cases of conflict between the government, as represented by the bureaucracy, and the aggrieved citizen. The office was slow in adoption outside Sweden, but eventually, with the growing complexity of society, ombudsmen were appointed in Finland (1919), Denmark (1953) and Norway (1963). Today New Zealand has an ombudsman whose functions are closely related to those of the Scandinavians; Great Britain and Japan have similar officers; and West Germany has an ombudsman whose sphere is limited to the military.

In social life, the general European upheaval of the sixties had a notable effect in Sweden. It strengthened the determination of the 'avant-garde right or wrong' element; more usefully, it created patterns of discussion even among Swedes who had previously thought there was nothing to talk about, let alone discuss. In addition, it started to break down the formality of Swedish life, and to put spontaneity before etiquette and custom.

A considerable amount of argument has been and continues to be based on the role of women in society. Probably nowhere else in Europe has the subject been more energetically and in general more rationally debated. The noisy excesses of Women's Liberation movements elsewhere have been largely avoided. An American writing in a Swedish journal summed the situation up with the remark: 'Instead of burning their bras [Swedish women] figured it was more practical to get their husbands to wash them out for them.' The debate has taken place against a background which contrives to combine the permissiveness portrayed in some well-known Swedish films with a stable and responsible family life which exists on a far larger scale. Sometimes, indeed, the two co-exist, as in the case of couples who, though perfectly responsible to each other and to their offspring, cannot bring themselves to sink to the bourgeois depths of even a civil marriage. For it they substitute what appears not much less bourgeois in form – the newspaper announcement of 'A Marriage of Conscience'. This procedure can be reconciled with a responsible attitude to the children because Sweden has been, since 1917, slowly eliminating the concept of illegitimacy. In 1970 all children born out of wedlock were given the legal right of inheritance.

The debate centres, as elsewhere, on equality of the sexes, but has been slanted more vigorously than elsewhere towards interchangeability of the sexes for all purposes except childbearing. Women can claim some notable successes, including a 27-year-old single girl who is a captain in the Merchant Navy; though the question whether, if she married, her husband would be allowed to sail with her, was not settled at the time of her appointment. The government has made its contribution on two levels. In the schools, both girls and boys learn woodwork and needlework, metal work and child care. Primarily for economic reasons – to get women out to work in a labour-scarce country – the tax allowance given to married men whose wives stay at home has been abolished, and husbands and working wives are now assessed entirely independently. This gesture, however, made in 1970, was not immediately accompanied by its practical complement – the provision of nurseries for every pre-school child. That remained a promise for the future.

In what is certainly an experimental period, no solution is ruled out of the discussion. If one of the parents is to take a part-time job in order to look after the children, it could as well be the father as the mother. If both parents are working, why not live in one of the new 'family hotels' where a day nursery and numerous other services are provided? This strengthens the impression gained by the outside observer that Sweden especially, and Scandinavia in general, could be moving towards a much more institutionalized way of life.

In the arts, the post-war decades have brought some radical changes in attitude and ambiance. Until 1945 Sweden had suffered from a certain provincialism, particularly in the visual arts, while writers and dramatists had been – and still are – inhibited by the smallness of the public whose mother tongue is Swedish. By now most of Swedish artistic output has become absorbed into an international style, and it has grown difficult to detect ideas which are either individually Swedish or outstandingly original. There is plenty of experiment, but little that could be considered exclusively Swedish.

Nevertheless, vitality is not lacking in any branch of the arts, partly as a result of the role in which society casts the artist, and the material help he receives. The artist or writer is a respected figure throughout the North, and in some cases more so than he deserves. Patronage, equally, has long been considered a public duty, to be dispensed on behalf of the population by central or local governments. A fairly extensive scheme of state bursaries has been developed in Sweden, and operates approximately at two levels. At one level, there are smallish bursaries payable for only a few years, principally to help the recipient to get on his feet. At the other, there are larger life pensions for established and deserving writers and artists, adjusted in proportion to the recipient's earnings. In addition, many smaller private forms of help are available, such as a house and endowment left to the Swedish Society of Authors to allow one of its members to live rent-free for an indefinite period.

For the outside world Swedish literature starts with social revolt. The banner was raised by August Strindberg (1849–1912), Sweden's greatest writer, although the escape from the earlier national romantic movement had already been heralded in the novels of the social critic and rebel, C. J. L. Almqvist (1793–1866). The disturbing and some-times disturbed genius Strindberg, with his mastery of the language and his power of ideas and their presentation, had a profound influence on later writers, though none has equalled him as a dramatist. To Strindberg and his Norwegian contemporary Henrik Ibsen (1828–1906), and to Ibsen's disciple Bernard Shaw, Europe owes much of the revival of the drama after its nineteenth-century decline. Also known outside Sweden in translation is the novelist Selma Lagerlöf (1858–1940), predominantly a fine storyteller. She was both the first woman and the first Swede to be awarded the Nobel Prize for Literature. Another Nobel prize-winner is Pär Lagerkvist (b. 1891) who is considered by many to be the greatest Swedish writer of his time. He stands out, not only by the quality of his writing, but more particularly by his preoccupation with the transcendental. In the Swedish secularized and post-Christian society, he is the only novelist to concern himself constantly with metaphysical questions. Two other well-known novelists of Lagerkvist's generation are Eyvind Johnson (b. 1900), and Wilhelm Moberg (b. 1898). Johnson made his name with books set against a Swedish proletarian background and enhanced it with a huge historical novel dealing with the age of Charlemagne, *Days of His Grace*. Moberg is known chiefly for a series of novels based on nineteenth-century Swedish emigration to the United States. A poet and novelist who established himself particularly in the post-war decade is Harry Martinson (b. 1904), whose long epic *Aniara* is a unique piece of science fiction transformed into profound poetry. It deals with the travellers in a spaceship which disappears into eternity, and has been made into an impressive opera by K.-B. Blomdahl.

The younger generation has responded to the winds of change by open concern over international and social issues, and by a more documentary treatment of those issues. It has set a belief in commitment against a form of 'faithlessness', which holds that society is changing so fast that no faith or belief can remain valid for long.

Scandinavia as a whole tends to excel in applied art (which is dealt with in another chapter) but is relatively weak in pure art, particularly painting. Sweden is no exception, although the work of a member of the royal family, Prince Eugen (1865–1947) is known and recognized outside Sweden. Much of Swedish painting is derived from folk culture, through either its primitive conception, or its portrayal of popular traditional life. Both Bror Hjorth (1894–1968) and Anders Zorn (1860–1920) have related themselves to folklore through their pictures of country life. Anders Zorn's home at Mora by Lake Siljan is a museum piece of his art and time. Bror Hjorth especially deals in a form of modern primitivism, in which he has been compared with Stanley Spencer. His wood sculpture, again primitive and sometimes more related to Africa than Sweden, has a power which underlines the need of a great number of Scandinavian artists to work in three dimensions. The modern generation appears to be following rather than originating international trends, while at the same time searching for a Swedish identity.

Among sculptors, Carl Milles (1875–1955) has been almost alone in earning a reputation outside Sweden. Greek-inspired, much of his output resulted from official commissions. In 'Milles' Garden', on the outskirts of Stockholm, a collection of his sculpture is displayed in the open air. Here his ability to convey a sense of movement and even flight, as in his trumpeting angels, becomes particularly evident.

Of all the arts, it is the cinema that has made Sweden known to the widest public abroad. For one generation Greta Garbo, for another Ingrid Bergman, the actress, and Ingmar Bergman, the director, have made an impact on people with otherwise little interest in Sweden. It is not surprising that the Swedes should have had so much success with films, for the alliance of art and technique, the scope for innovation and the absence of need for the kind of subtlety required by the theatre all accord with their natural endowment. Since Ingmar Bergman, Alf Sjöberg and Arne Sucksdorff made their notable films of the forties and fifties, the rest of the world has realized that it cannot ignore the Swedish cinema. After them have come another generation of directors – among them Bo Widerberg, Vilgot Sjöman and Jan Troell – eager to experiment and explore. Although Bergman and Sjöberg have also turned their attention successfully to the theatre, their productions suggest that the natural dramatic element of the Swedes is less the theatre than the cinema.

Sweden today is the pacemaker of Scandinavia. The aggressive and expansionist military and political policies of past centuries now belong to history, but the spirit which inspired them has found other means of expression, even in the context of a longstanding neutrality. Industrially, socially, and often personally, there is a deliberate forward thrust, a determined ambition to be in the vanguard of the twentieth century. The Swedes themselves speak of 'royal Swedish envy' as one of their characteristics, and this may act as an additional spur to their ambition. Keeping up with the Swedes has thus become a general Scandinavian preoccupation, for better and for worse. It can overstrain the resources of the less prosperous, or divert them from fields where they can excel over the Swedes. But to Sweden every other Nordic country owes something of the urge to advance, expand and experiment which has served them so well in this century.

Part Three   The Scandinavian contribution

10   Social laboratories

IN MODERN TIMES the Scandinavian countries have acquired a particular reputation both for their social services and their social security. They have been regarded as 'social laboratories' where experiments in the welfare of human beings were pursued and pioneering work conducted. Non-Scandinavians of right-wing persuasion have often condemned their systems as arrant socialism, disregarding the fact that many advances in the social field have been made by right-wing governments. Social services in the Northern countries have sprung from a social conscience and a community instinct rather than from ideological intent. Inevitably politicians have at times given them a political twist, and the tendency latterly has been to accentuate political considerations, particularly as the cost of social security rises and politico-economic factors become increasingly important. There is little significant disagreement about the extent or nature of the social services; dispute and doubt centre rather on the ability of each country to devote so high a percentage of its gross national product to social security.

Occasionally, the impression is gained that social security and welfare were invented in Scandinavia. It is true that a few individual aspects of the system have a long history. By 1800, for instance, Sweden had twenty-one hospitals, for all of which the state and the provinces were responsible. But in the introduction of a comprehensive social security scheme, the Northern countries were well outpaced by Germany in the early nineteenth century. In 1933, Denmark introduced what was then considered the most comprehensive social legislation in the world. The British National Insurance Act of 1948 went, at that time, further than anything comparable in Scandinavia, particularly in the provision of health services. By now, however, most of the Nordic countries have caught up with or gone beyond Britain, although there are differences of emphasis, not only between Britain and Scandinavia, but among the Scandinavian countries themselves.

Reciprocity of certain social benefits throughout the Northern countries began as far back as 1907, and has since developed steadily. But benefits are neither equal nor uniform in all five countries. (For this reason, it is impossible to deal systematically with all the provisions of all five countries in this chapter. Only general trends and a limited number of instances can be given.) A Swede living in Norway could not, at present, draw his retirement pension until the age of 70, but would be eligible in Sweden for a considerably larger pension at 67. On the other hand, there is a valuable pooling of resources in the more specialized services. If, to take one example, a retarded or handicapped Finnish boy cannot get exactly the education he needs in Finland, he can go to a special school in Sweden without having to pay any fees.

All five Nordic countries provide the basic forms of security common to most western European countries: unemployment and sickness benefit, maternity benefit and family allowances, retirement pensions and health services (the last not entirely free). For Iceland in particular, with its small population, this is a sizeable achievement; but it cannot provide some specialized forms of treatment – and it is an expensive journey to mainland Scandinavia. What makes the social framework in the North interesting to the outsider is the scope for fresh thinking and experiment provided in countries with smaller populations, the possibilities of certain forms of selectivity, and the appeal to personal responses and responsibility.

A crucial point is the central involvement of the local authority. In Denmark, Finland and Sweden, the communes are obliged to appoint a director of social welfare to unify the health and social services at a local level. Even in Helsinki, with its half-million inhabitants, a director has said that it was possible to survey and co-ordinate services so that the vast majority received their just due and few got the chance to abuse the system. In a smaller community it is obviously easier still to operate to the best advantage of the individual. The fairly low rates of unemployment at present in Scandinavia also eliminate some of the more difficult problems, and enable a firm line to be taken.

Nowhere may an unemployed man refuse suitable work offered and continue to draw benefit. Equally, if he takes a job and leaves it without good cause he ceases to be eligible for benefit. In Denmark benefits are withheld from strikers, on the grounds that labour conflicts cannot be continued at the taxpayer's expense. In many cases an unemployed young and able-bodied man must agree to re-training; often others must remove to areas where work is available, when they will be given removal and re-establishment grants. Sometimes assistance may be given partly in kind – a sewing-machine or a set of tools, for instance – which will increase a worker's earning potential. There is a certain amount of supervision of the way cash assistance is used; if – and rarely – it is totally misused, it may take the form of an order to a tradesman to deliver goods regularly.

In social benefits, as in so many other spheres, the Swedes are the pacemakers and as such tend to aggravate the economic problems of the rest of Scandinavia. A currently tender spot is the retirement pension. In Sweden this is a basic sum, on the generous side, tied to the economic index. But in addition there is a supplementary pension, the equivalent of 60 per cent of the average income during the pensioner's fifteen most remunerative years, minus the basic sum. Not unnaturally, workers in the other Northern countries have demanded similar pensions. Denmark and Finland cannot immediately afford anything on this scale. Norway may manage it, though with 70 as the pensionable age, as against 67 in Sweden. But in the end, the pressure may be such that every country will have to fall in line with Sweden.

The provision of the health services is also rather more generous in Sweden than elsewhere in Scandinavia, though nowhere are they completely free. The patient pays a percentage of the doctor's fee and the cost of drugs. In Norway and Sweden all hospital treatment in public wards is free, but in other countries there is a small charge. Most hospitals are maintained by local authorities at a high standard, and a 'public ward' usually means a pleasant room with four to six beds. Even in Sweden the patient pays all his own dental charges.

Finland deserves a special mention in view of the extent of its private welfare measures. State social services developed late, partly owing to the late date of Finnish independence (1917). But long before then, industrial firms had regarded it as their proper duty to care for the welfare of their employees, both in and out of working hours. The location of a factory has generally depended on the proximity of water, either as a source of power, or a means of transport for timber. Therefore the workers had to come to the factory and the factory had to provide for the community – its homes, its schools, its medical care, its leisure activities. In many parts of the country there are big industrial concerns which come close to pampering the worker – even to the extent of giving a few of the best free trips to the United States. These private welfare schemes were already well developed before state social services became available, and now the workers, not surprisingly, want to hang on to the private as well as state services. This creates an overall inequality, as other workers, particularly those in agriculture and forestry, generally lack paternal employers to look after their welfare.

Since the war housing has presented the Northern countries with a special challenge. The pre-war situation, in terms of space occupancy, was anything but good. In Paris at that time it was not unusual to find an upper middle-class family of three living in the magnificent squalor of an old eight- or ten-roomed flat. In Stockholm precisely opposing conditions prevailed. The flat might be modern, well-planned and 'well-appointed' – but three people lived in its two smallish rooms and thought themselves lucky not to have to squeeze, like many families, into a one-room flat. All over the North, and particularly in Sweden and Finland, there was high occupancy, often to the point of overcrowding, but at least there was nothing approaching the slums of other west European countries.

During the war there was relatively little building, but also relatively little destruction, except in Finnish and Norwegian Lapland. The internal migration from countryside to towns which followed the rapid pace of post-war industrialization was responsible for the real dimensions of the housing problem. The population of many towns has doubled since the war. For several years after the war severe rationing schemes were enforced, and families had to accept such accommodation as authority decided, whether they liked it or not. Only fairly recently has a greater element of choice developed – though often by the purse – and the town-dweller has ceased to feel imprisoned for all time within walls he may not like. Enforced immobility is a great hardship for many Scandinavians, for whom a removal is often a highly pleasurable event.

The problem was, and still is, accentuated by the high cost of building in a cold climate. Deep foundations, thermal installations, insulation, and double or triple glazing are expensive necessities, while the old custom of building only in warm weather was both uneconomic and hopelessly slow. Fortunately, new techniques which speed building and enable work to continue throughout the winter have eased at least that difficulty.

Surprisingly, Iceland, where the housing problem was most acute of all, has come through the post-war trials the most successfully. Possibly there was relatively more to be done here than elsewhere in Scandinavia, since the old wooden houses with their corrugated iron roofs had to be replaced by new concrete buildings. By dint of spending a higher percentage of the GNP on housing than any other Northern country, Iceland eventually claimed a slight housing surplus. In addition, it built a higher proportion of larger dwelling units than the other Scandinavian countries, although they too were beginning to break out of their previously limited confines. And in few places did the 'rags to riches' story develop so rapidly and dramatically. Iceland did not merely build large concrete dwellings; it fitted them out with washing-machines and refrigerators, and harnessed its natural hot springs to provide central heating. All new dwellings have central heating, and forty per cent of them, including the entire city of Reykjavik, have geothermal heating drawn from Iceland's hot springs.

Visitors to the larger Scandinavian towns inevitably receive the impression that the majority of people live in flats. Certainly the trend is markedly in this direction, particularly in Finland and Sweden, but least of all in Norway. But where planners have had at their disposal a fairly large area to build or re-build, they have frequently attempted to vary both the types and sizes of dwelling and their visual aspect. The more advanced planning authorities insist on creating the conditions for a mixed and integrated society. They include, within a small radius, family-size houses or flats in small blocks, small flats in tower blocks for single people, and provision for old people. The last frequently takes the form of a purpose-built block, where everything is planned to simplify the life of an elderly person. Denmark, however, where so much pioneering in housing for the old has been done, has now moved away from the idea of the single block occupied only by the elderly. Instead, the ground-floor flats of new blocks are frequently planned and equipped for the old, and the provision of such flats may often be the condition of the granting of a subsidy to the building organization.

Equally, the hiving-off of housing according to income group or occupation, never very frequent, is becoming increasingly rare. By and large, only the size of a newish dwelling reflects the occupant's ability to pay. Situation, amenities and standards of building and equipment are likely to be the same whether the occupant is the managing director or an unskilled labourer.

The creation of a socially mixed community is made easier by the policy, followed all over Scandinavia, of subsidizing the occupant rather than the dwelling. The precise form and amount of the subsidy varies from country to country, and occasionally from town to town within a single country. Sweden was the first to introduce such subsidies, in 1935, and today provides them more extensively than the other Nordic countries. In general, subsidies are given only to families with one or more children under sixteen, and to elderly people with low incomes.

In addition, loans to enable more people to buy their homes are readily made available by governments on easy terms, and ownership, whether of a house or a flat, has for many years been more usual than elsewhere in Europe. Single-family houses are almost always owner-occupied; and ownership of flats has been facilitated by the variety of approach to multi-family housing. Co-operatives and other non-profit-making housing societies have a longish history in Denmark, and have spread quickly to the other Northern countries. Only in Sweden has post-war municipal building outstripped any other form, and even here the form is indirect. Thus homes may be built by a non-profit-making society which is owned by the municipality, but has a certain independence and freedom of action.

In Finland a few big industrial firms help their employees to build their own homes with loans, large-scale purchase of materials and generous advice to the handy who can do part of the work themselves and often save 15 to 20 per cent of the total cost in the process. But the general Scandinavian trend is in the opposite direction. The cost of new dwellings reaching officially required standards is now so high that few families could live in them without a subsidy in some form or other.

The relatively cramped living conditions of the North and the preponderance of flats in the bigger cities have meant that young and old have lacked the space for all but sedentary leisure pursuits. Fortunately, public reaction has been to provide more opportunities for constructive leisure, particularly for children and young people. Many of these provisions serve the additional purpose of taking care of the children of working mothers during the period between the end of school hours and office or factory hours. One of the simplest and cheapest institutions is that of the 'park aunt'. (All adults, known and unknown, are 'Aunt' or 'Uncle' to Scandinavian children.) The park aunt, paid by the municipality, operates in parks and public gardens, supervising children aged between a few months and seven years. Mothers pay a small amount in return, can leave their children in the morning or the afternoon, and must fetch them as soon as it starts to rain. Otherwise the park aunt is on duty all the year round, and only when the temperature drops below 15°F, is it thought too cold for the children to play out of doors.

For schoolchildren there are free-time or recreation centres where they may do their homework and play after school hours and in school holidays. In the holidays these centres often provide hot meals for the children of working mothers. Denmark, which pioneered the adventure playground, involving inevitably a certain and perhaps necessary amount of destruction, has also pioneered the construction playground, where both boys and girls can learn to build sheds, carts and other simple objects.

The establishment of youth clubs and centres for young people between about twelve and twenty has been the official and semi-official response to the increase in juvenile delinquency which has not spared Scandinavia, although it has taken somewhat less violent forms than elsewhere. In Sweden the municipality is responsible for the provision of such centres, although it may delegate their day-to-day running to local associations. On the whole, this is a field in which Scandinavia profits by the scarcity of purely voluntary enterprise, particularly of the do-good type which aims, often so fruitlessly, at direct conversion and reform. The Scandinavian clubs offer a variety of activities, among which young people may make their own choice. For instance, a Swedish centre in an area with a population of 10,000 may include a café, a hall for sports, gymnastics and dancing, a larger hall for special programmes, theatre and films, hobby-rooms, club-rooms and study-rooms. The Danes offer, in their larger centres, up to twenty-five different types of hobbies and recreational activities. Often premises are purpose-built, particularly in new suburban housing developments, and almost always they are gay and inviting.

In Copenhagen there is a special institution, the Kofoed School, which takes in homeless, rootless and often semi-delinquent young men between eighteen and twenty-five, often by invitation during nightly searches of the town by the School's welfare officers. It aims at rehabilitating and re-training by a system of rewards for effort and co-operation, and eventually sending them out better equipped to face the world and earn a living.

The prison population in Scandinavia is relatively low, though increasing; partly, perhaps, because of a lower criminal tendency, partly because of a more lenient attitude (except towards drunken drivers, on whom the severity of the law falls mercilessly). But once a man is inside, he is treated as rationally as possible within the context of his crime. He can do useful work and be paid for it, often at market rates, from which compensation for injury done and savings for release are deducted. In the Helsinki prison, for instance, are made all the number plates for cars used in Finland. Sweden has inaugurated many experiments, several aimed at keeping long-sentence prisoners in some form of contact with the outside world. Particularly interesting is the small prison in the ancient university town of Uppsala. Here prisoners are enabled to continue their education, some at the university itself, and are helped in their studies by regular university students.

That these and other educational facilities should be available to prisoners is hardly surprising in Scandinavia, given the importance there attached to learning. The Northern countries are properly known for the quality and breadth of their educational systems – an achievement all the more remarkable when viewed against the small size of each country and their poverty, or, at best, limited resources in the nineteenth century when the system of public education was built up. However, the respect, even veneration, for education stretches back to the Lutheran reformation, with its insistence on the power and importance of learning. Still today in Denmark, Finland and Norway, education and religious affairs are dealt with in single ministries of Church and Education. The Church no longer wields any influence in the totally secularized educational systems of the present day; the ministries remain as a reminder of the time when mind and spirit were treated, and sometimes exploited, in interaction. Typically, Bishop Gezelius in Finland was largely responsible for the law of 1686, by which a Finn who could not read was not allowed to make his first communion or get married. King Christian VI of Denmark issued in 1739 a decree introducing compulsory education for all children, to be undertaken principally by deacons, and with the intention of using schools as a means of promoting religious ideals. The cathedral school in Bergen recalls the religious origins of the oldest schools. Scholarliness replaced cleanliness in the ladder to godliness.

This quasi-religious attitude to education led, in the nineteenth century, to the adoption of free and compulsory state schooling decades before Britain took the same step in 1870. When the union of Denmark and Norway was dissolved in 1814, Denmark immediately introduced compulsory state education; Norway followed in 1827 and Sweden in 1842. In the Grand Duchy of Finland, primary education occasioned fruitful debate, and from 1866 onwards became general. The absence of any desire or opportunity for private schooling (today only about 3 per cent of pupils in Denmark, Norway and Sweden attend private schools) eased the development of state schools. Since almost the entire populations of the Nordic countries are Lutheran, and since the Lutheran Church does not, like the Roman Catholic Church in other countries, compete with secular schools, the state has been able to develop education unhampered by religious conflict. But the Lutheran Church did emphasize the role to be played by parents in the education of their children, and this still remains part of the Northern tradition. If today education has become totally secularized, it commands no less a degree of respect. 'Professor' remains one of the most envied of titles or appellations.   The standard of teaching is so high that many secondary school teachers eventually become university lecturers or professors. Swedish school teachers are among the most highly paid in the world.

The weakness of Scandinavian schooling, until fairly recently, was its short length. In no Nordic country does compulsory education begin before the age of seven; until the reforms and re-organizations of the years after the Second World War it lasted only until fourteen (fifteen in Finland), although pupils could and did stay on several years longer. In post-war developments the Swedes have, as in other spheres, forced the pace; the other Nordic countries are more cautiously following them, and developing on similar, though not identical lines. There is still a certain reluctance to go all the way with Sweden in either its declared conviction that 'in the creation of an egalitarian and democratic society, the educational system occupies a central position', or in the importance it attaches to uniformity.

The new Swedish system, briefly, is as follows: all children must attend a nine-year course in a single comprehensive-type co-educational school, between the ages of seven and sixteen. There is no streaming or other form of division of classes, which may not have more than 25 pupils in the first three years, or 30 in the following six years. From the seventh year onwards pupils are allowed a measure of choice of subjects. After the ninth year pupils go on to the 'gymnasium', where they stay at least three years. Traditionally, in Germany and Scandinavia, the gymnasium has always been a school which prepared older pupils for the university, and enjoyed particular prestige. In Sweden, as elsewhere, non-academic pupils could continue their education at professional and vocational schools. Now Sweden alone has changed the traditional character of the gymnasium by making it comprehensive and merging with it the professional and vocational schools. It has been alone in abolishing the 'student examination', taken at the end of the gymnasium course, and qualifying successful candidates for entry to the university. Now any student who has completed a course of study in a gymnasium is eligible for university education.

Whether this egalitarian turn will lead to any dilution of the gymnasium's hitherto exceptionally high standards of scholarship is yet to be seen; but various modifications of the original comprehensive system became quickly necessary, and it still is far from lacking in critics. What appears relatively certain is that the number of Swedish pupils staying on at school until nineteen, twenty or even twenty-one will increase steadily. In 1950 cash grants were made available to parents whose children stayed at school beyond the compulsory nine years. By 1970 85 per cent of pupils were still at school after the years of compulsion were over, and Sweden claimed a higher rate of success than the United States in keeping pupils at school until they reached a considerable pre-academic standard.

It cannot yet be foreseen how far the other Scandinavian countries will go in emulation of the new Swedish system. Certainly Norway and Denmark are likely to adopt the nine-year comprehensive school, but less likely to make post-compulsory education comprehensive. At the time when the school-leaving age was still fourteen, the Danes introduced an interesting and productive measure. Any child who left school at fourteen was welcomed back unconditionally if he decided to return a year later. The numbers who did so decide were considerable. Either they realized how meagre their qualifications were, or they found the outside world too harsh, or both.

In Finland historical development has created a totally different system of secondary education. When Finland was part of Sweden, and for much of the century when it was a Grand Duchy of Russia, only the Swedish language was used in state schools. Finnish-language schools were set up on private initiative, with the result that today there are twice as many private or communally-owned as state secondary schools. Private schools, nevertheless, receive 80 per cent of their running costs from the state. They are obliged to follow, with minor variations, the same curricula as state schools, and to comply with state regulations and standards. However, their existence has created some of the more subtle distinctions with which the British are familiar. Parents know which private schools have turned out well-known public figures, and which are more specialized in certain fields of studies. In the bigger towns they have a degree of choice, provided they can pay the fees, which are considerably higher than those still charged in state secondary schools. But elsewhere in Scandinavia choice may be completely absent. However, in spite of their very individual educational system, the Finns are now moving slowly in the direction of the comprehensive school.

Secondary education becomes a heavy financial burden on the community in the thinly peopled northern areas, where boarding facilities (non-existent farther south in Scandinavia) are indispensable. Instruction for minorities is also a feature of the high north, where there are special Lapp schools. Among the best-known are those at Karasjokk and Jokkmokk, where traditional arts and crafts form a lively part of the curriculum. Denmark has its own peculiar educational responsibilities for the Eskimos of Greenland. The teaching of handicrafts was well established in Scandinavian schools by the end of the nineteenth century. Physical education also evolved against the background of firm pedagogic philosophies, and in both these spheres Scandinavia became a centre of influence in its own right. Vocational training has a solid foundation. Nowhere are there better agricultural schools for smallholders, dairy schools for dairy farmers (and dairy maids) and forestry schools for forest farmers. As with old-established university courses in these subjects, extended spells of practical work on recognized farms are a required part of the training.

For decades, even centuries, university education in Scandinavia has been characterized by its thoroughness and its length. Until recently it was difficult to obtain a first degree in the three or four years usually allowed elsewhere in Europe. The tendency now is to complete the course in approximately this length of time. Nevertheless the willingness to spend several years studying, when it is normal to enter a university at twenty or twenty-one, is remarkable. It is made all the more so by the practice of financing studies through loans which have to be paid back in later life. Some mitigation corresponds with circumstances: a missionary, for instance, would not be expected to pay back a loan in full; a successful industrialist would.

Also remarkable is the early date at which universities were established in Scandinavia. The University of Uppsala in Sweden was founded in 1477, two years before the University of Copenhagen, and rapidly acquired the international reputation it has enjoyed ever since. Lund, Sweden's second university, was founded in 1668. In Finland, the University of Turku (1640) had also gained high international esteem long before it moved to Helsinki when the latter became the Finnish capital. Oslo's university came into being in 1811, and the University of Iceland in 1911. Since the war more than a dozen new universities have been established – the northernmost in Umeå (with more than 10,000 students) and Oulu. Each country has schemes for further expansion. Denmark, for example, plans university centres in Roskilde, Aalborg and Ribe-Esbjerg. Nevertheless, pressure for places remains acute, and constitutes a political issue. Norway's capacity for training doctors and dentists, for instance, is so far below requirements that scores of young Norwegians are now being trained in the medical and dental schools of the north of England and Scotland.

Yet despite the pressure on places and the number of applicants who must be turned down, the percentage of the school population going on to the university is high. It has at times been higher in Sweden and Finland than anywhere else in Europe. A somewhat disheartening feature is that the difficulty in getting into a university may, at certain times and in certain countries, be paralleled by a difficulty in getting a suitable job afterwards. In small countries the number of good jobs available is bound to be limited, and arts graduates in particular may run into employment problems. On the other hand, the high technological expertise of the Scandinavians has made a vast contribution to the industrial success of small countries dependent on international trade.

There has been student unrest in Scandinavia, but on the whole it has not taken violent forms. All the Northern countries are experimenting with ways of giving both secondary school pupils and students more say in the running of schools and higher educational establishments; radical pressure for one-man-one-vote (from principal to caretaker) in university management is strong. But an already important aspect of student participation is the extent to which students have, for many years, been expected to shoulder responsibility.

In summer vacation months hostels frequently become tourist hotels run by the students themselves. Some hostels have been financed by students' efforts and are run by them all the year round. Finnish students have been notably active in this respect. The Students' Union of the Technical University of Helsinki itself financed the building of its splendid headquarters, and proceeded to pay off the mortgage by letting them out for international conferences and smart night life. Other young Finns run restaurants in Helsinki, and some have initiated trade exhibitions abroad. So it is rightly observed that, whatever academic subjects they may have studied, many students come out of the university with no small business experience.

All over Scandinavia, there are very considerable opportunities of further education for those who have not been to the university, or not even had more than seven years' schooling. Evening classes and short summer courses are numerous and well-attended. But most interesting and distinctively Scandinavian are the 'Folk High Schools' originated by Bishop Grundtvig of Denmark in the 1830s. The Scandinavians, incidentally, when speaking or writing in English, all make the literal translation from *folkhögskola* (Swedish) to 'folk high school'. This is a misleading term to Anglo-Saxons, since students cannot attend a folk high school until the years of normal schooling are over.

Grundtvig's object was to provide in these schools the kind of liberal though informal education which would simultaneously foster the development of the individual's character and his potentialities as a citizen. Throughout the century which followed, folk high schools of varying types were established, developed and changed in certain respects, but never lost the original basis formulated by Grundtvig. Today in Denmark alone there are nearly seventy folk high schools, attended annually by about eight thousand students. The majority are privately owned, often by local groups, larger organizations, or national movements such as a religious body or a political party. No educational qualifications are required, but no student under eighteen is accepted. Generally, students are between twenty and twenty-five, and have left school at fourteen. The courses vary in length from five or six months in winter (when agricultural workers in pre-industrial Denmark could most easily leave the farms) through three-month courses to more exceptional two-week summer holiday courses. All folk high schools are residential, and considerable store is set by contacts between teachers and taught, and between the students themselves. Subjects most commonly taught, through lectures and study groups, are Danish language and literature, history, civics and economics, mathematics, science, world literature, foreign languages, psychology, international affairs and art. A certain number, by contrast, are more specialized in curricula or students. There are, for instance, nursing high schools and high schools catering specially for fishermen.

The benefits of folk high school courses are so evident that a high proportion of industrial employers are ready to release their employees, and pay their fees and part or all of their wages while they are at a folk high school. Now a great many married couples follow courses together, most schools being co-educational. The benefits to the community are equally evident; it has been generally observed that those who most frequently take the lead in local and voluntary affairs are ex-students of folk high schools.

The folk high school movement spread rapidly to the other Scandinavian countries, which all, in the nineteenth century, had the comparable rural communities for whom such schools had particular value. In any over-all assessment of their influence there are innumerable imponderables. But it would not be unjustified to believe that the particular type of education given by folk high schools has made a significant contribution to the relatively smooth transition from agricultural to industrial societies, and to the more reasonable, if still imperfect, state of labour relations in the North.

The development of the social services in Scandinavia will inevitably be conditioned by the varying attitudes of each individual country. Among the psychological variants, for instance, is the extent of voluntary participation, nowhere very large, and in Sweden smallest of all. Sweden having been the leader in the past, its influence may remain powerful in determining attitudes as well as actions. The Swedish attitude is often vigorously rational and humanist, and has been strongly influenced in its development by both Keynes and Beveridge. The emphasis is placed constantly on *rights,* and on the non-relation to charity in any form. A further emphasis is placed on the *rightness* of social security, and includes, at a certain age-level, an unwillingness to question or doubt its principles, although the details of its practice are under frequent review. A senior civil servant working in the Swedish Ministry of Health and Social Affairs has commented: 'The individual's demand for security and social care rises with his affluence. Once a high standard of living has been achieved, there is more reason to aim at greater security than at further increases in the standard. The man who has much to lose has correspondingly much to protect.'

This is a reaction fairly common to the individuals and groups, political and social, who fought for security against the insecure background of the thirties. Today a younger generation, without experience of that insecurity, is beginning to take over. Although its views are as yet incompletely formed or formulated, it questions the merit of hard work (which has in the past paid for social security); it lays more emphasis than its elders on equality of effort and reward. Thus the influence of this generation on the evolution of social security in Sweden, and in Scandinavia as a whole, is unforeseeable. Much depends on economic development, on the extent to which prosperity becomes more evenly distributed over the North. In the social field, as in many others, the seventies may well bring changes more radical than those contained in the gradualism of past decades.

11   The art of design

In the process of post-war vulgarization, the words 'Scandinavian design' have come to connote, outside the North, almost any object in domestic use which is simple and modern, whatever its source or its merits. Even those of more discerning eye tend to regard the design of Scandinavia as a twentieth-century phenomenon, instead of the development of a gift for craftsmanship and line which goes back beyond Viking times. The ship burials and other archeological finds of more than a thousand years ago have revealed jewellery and metal objects, sometimes primitive, sometimes small works of art. More significantly, the vessels themselves, such as the Oseberg and Gokstad ships, which belong to the ninth century and can be seen in Oslo, are of a shapeliness which has never been surpassed. They are built with so great a sense of flow and rhythm that music and poetry seem to blend in ships also so seaworthy as to be capable of voyages as long as many taken by the liners of today. Not all the ships which carried the Vikings to distant lands could have shared these qualities, but they played their part in a development of design which has continued into this century.

From Spain and Morocco the Vikings brought home knotted wool rugs which were eventually copied by their womenfolk in Norway, Sweden and Finland. Called *rya* in Norway and Sweden, and *ryijy* in Finland, they covered, in their plain, utilitarian versions, floors and beds and lined sleighs. In Norway and Sweden the *rya* disappeared, but in Finland it became one of the most admired and prized of the works of the hand. The Finnish woman's zest for colour and design transformed it into a wallhanging, a poor man's tapestry, often treated as an heirloom. Today the *ryijy* has been revived and developed artistically and commercially. Designers in Finland, and to a lesser extent in the other Scandinavian countries, have treated it as an art form, making it overflow with fantasy and colour in a way which could be thought impossible in a rug. These artist-designed *ryijy* are as expensive as many modern French tapestries, but machine-made versions are now on sale in many countries.

The centuries-old story of the *ryijy* is in many ways the story of Scandinavian design, especially in its opposition and relation to Western European design. In Scandinavia domestic design was essentially simple, inexpensive, adapted to its purpose, and suited to the daily lives of ordinary people. The traditions of most of Western Europe, on the other hand, had stemmed from the Renaissance, and so the designs of the domestic interior were based on a gorgeousness to which only noble and aristocratic families with a retinue of servants could aspire. They were dependent for their execution on artists and craftsmen of high calibre, whose work could rarely be translated to the machine when the industrial revolution and the ensuing ugliness of mass production took over.

So Western Europe, faced in the twentieth century with the simpler way of life imposed by smaller dwellings and an absence of servants, had little to turn to or adapt within its own traditions. In Scandinavia, on the other hand, domestic design had evolved gradually to meet the needs of the day. The Northern countries, poor, untouched by the industrial revolution, and largely uninfluenced by the decorative glories of Italy and France, had continued in their homespun way. For most of their inhabitants, living in the remote countryside, the ordinary objects of everyday life were unobtainable, whether afford-able or not. But most of them, equally, had the hand and eye for purposeful creativity, and could supply their own needs in a way that was always practical and frequently beautiful. There were manu-facturing exceptions, the most famous among them the Royal Copenhagen porcelain factory which was established in 1775. Already then the faience factory of Rörstrand in Sweden had been at work for half a century, and claims today to be the oldest of its kind in Europe in terms of continuous production. In the seventeen hund-reds, too, small glass works were set up in Finland, Norway and Sweden.

However, the true bases of most Scandinavian design were wood and wool. Except in Denmark, there was wood on the doorstep of every yeoman and peasant farmer, and from it he could fashion almost all that he needed. Wood built his home and his barns, his plough, wagon, sleigh, skis and boat. It built his furniture, sometimes in the gently decorative style known as 'peasant baroque', sometimes simpler in line and brightly and naively painted. And after furniture came all the smaller, lesser necessities: the wooden platters and tankards, the moulds in which cheese hardened, the spoons, forks, and ladles. He took even strips of birch bark and plaited them into shoes and baskets, while straw was twisted into fanciful and decorative shapes. All these things he made with an apparently innate sense of line and proportion – and continued to make and use them when the rest of Europe had turned to machine-made goods.

Among the most important of the countryman's products were the spinning wheel and loom which he made for his wife. Outside in the shippen a few sheep lived in greater fear of the shears than the oven, able to provide the family with warm coverings and clothing. Sometimes a patch of flax provided linen and hemp fishing nets. The countrywoman of the North was as gifted in the handling of wool and linen as was her husband in the fashioning of wood. As well as *rya*, she made clothes and bed and table linen, and developed colourful pictorial wall decorations, doubly and intricately woven from coarse linen thread.

It was not only the gifted eye and hand which made the crafts of the North significant. Equally important was the esteem in which they were held. There was something akin, in the Northern home, to the English garden. The poor man might well grow a more beautiful rose than the rich man, and the rich man did not begrudge him his success. Still today, in the North, no one is surprised when an untaught girl on a remote farm produces an outstanding piece of handweaving. Most of the population has a natural appreciation, inherited over the centuries, of what is good or bad in design.

Besides, the home was, and still is, the centre of daily life in a more distinctive way than in any other country in the western world. It was not only that Scandinavia lacked the cafés, clubs and pubs of other countries; the home was the psychological as well as the physical defence against the climate. For days, even weeks, of winter the windows of a house in the country might look out upon an unchanging, bare, grey-white or darkening expanse of snow. The spontaneous reaction of the housewife was to change something in the house – to make new curtains, a new cushion, a new tablecloth. For her it was the tonic equivalent to the new hat or dress bought by women farther west and south. Today the love of variety and change persists, even among town-dwellers no longer psychologically imprisoned by chill and gloom. The Northern woman frequently possesses an unusual amount of china, glass and table linen, so that she can ring the changes in style and colour; and she buys according to her fancy, and not when the cups are broken or the tablecloth torn. Thus a flourishing 'home market', in its most literal sense, exists for domestic design.

As a result of good fortune and sound instinct, the handicrafts of the North were allowed neither to die away nor to become divorced from daily life when the machines began to take over. As early as 1845 the Swedish Society of Industrial Design was founded, the first of its kind in the world. The Finnish Society of Crafts and Design followed in 1875, and corresponding Danish and Norwegian societies were established in 1907 and 1918. The primary aim of all these societies is, naturally, the encouragement of good design in everyday life, and of the principal means to that end – the participation of the artist in industry. At the same time they have helped to maintain and often modernize traditional home crafts, and, at the other end of the scale, to promote the production of individual pieces of glass, ceramics, silver and other materials which rank as works of art in their own right. 'Industrial art', an expert has observed, 'is to Scandinavia what painting is to France and music to Germany.'

Crucial to the work of these societies was and is a visually enlightened and interested public. The existing number of gifted amateurs could have been expected to supply such a public, but in fact, Gresham's law has threatened to operate at times even in Scandinavia. There are philistines around in every decade and generation; at times machines have produced appalling cheap goods, whose only alternative was the highly expensive handmade; and at times some very big blind spots have been discovered in the most enlightened of firms. Nevertheless, there are throughout the North far greater numbers of people than elsewhere whose normal conversation includes comment on new designs, whether of a water tower or a roll of shelf paper. The shelf paper is one of the clues to the widening general interest in design. The Scandinavians have designed first and foremost for everyday life, and artists have not considered shelf paper unworthy of their attention. Thus even people of very slender means have had some small stimulus to their interest in and observation of things around them.

It is not easy to pinpoint a date at which industrial design came of age, as it were, in Scandinavia. From about 1925 it began to be known, through international exhibitions, to a limited public outside the North, and continued to develop gradually. Well before the Second World War, Alvar Aalto's furniture and Georg Jensen's silver, to name two products particularly well known at that time, were being exported on a small scale to a number of foreign countries. But it was in the post-war years, particularly in the period between about 1950 and 1965, that an explosion of creativity and invention took place in the Northern countries. The Design Societies played an important part in this period of outstanding success. They were frequently instrumental in persuading manufacturers to employ artist-designers, and, most significant, to employ them in total freedom. Their success was particularly evident in firms manufacturing china and glass. In a single firm a dozen or so designers would all have their own studios, where they could experiment freely with either expensive decorative pieces or designs suited for mass production. Many of the prizes won by Scandinavians at the Milan Triennali (aptly dubbed by a Finnish expert 'the Olympic Games of Design') were gained by pieces created in the security and freedom of these factory studios.

By now Scandinavian domestic design is so well known that its major characteristics are more or less taken for granted. The rest of the world has forgotten that Nordic designers were among the first to insist on fitness for purpose and circumstances. Chairs designed scientifically to fit the human anatomy and allow it to maintain the right posture were first developed in Denmark in the nineteen-twenties. In Sweden a great deal of research has gone into functional aspects such as the best height for tables, the best size and shape for beds. (The last badly needed; until fairly recently a comfortable bed was a luxury rarely found in Scandinavia.) Nor is it easy to remember that the Danish firm of Georg Jensen, one of the world's great silver-smiths, were the innovators, in the immediate post-war years, of stainless steel tableware. Typically, their designers recognized the need of the times, were not too proud to work in a baser metal, and were prepared to ride out the storm of conservative disgust which greeted their earlier designs, though as elegant in their simplicity as much that had been done by the firm in silver. Since then, although stainless steel has been adopted to a greater or lesser degree all over the world, the Scandinavians are still pre-eminent in its design.

It was hardly difficult for the Scandinavians to design for the post-war circumstances of smaller homes and absent help, because they were accustomed to living in small compass, and unused to butlers and the more pretentious forms of servantry. Wine glasses on feet that could be stacked one inside the other did not look particularly revolutionary when the Finns first designed them – but apparently no one had thought of such a thing before. Nor had the Europeans learnt to use walls for any furniture other than bookshelves before the Scandinavians developed their multi-purpose and space-saving wall units. These were only two of a host of practical ideas which made home furnishing and housekeeping easier.

Above all, in its golden age between 1950 and 1965, Scandinavian design was characterized by absence of clutter, purity of line and excellence of proportion. Sometimes, it is true, and particularly in its less colourful phase, it seemed a little too ascetic or anaemic, a little too close to what has been called 'ghastly good taste'. Indeed, to furnish entirely in modern Scandinavian has proved too taxing for the majority of Scandinavian home-makers themselves. They have recognized the dangers of impersonality, even uniformity, in furniture particularly, and prefer to blend old and new wherever they can.

One of the great common characteristics of Scandinavian design is something invisible in the immediate sense of the word, but of paramount importance – the versatility of the designer, and hence, more often than not, his ability to see a building, a room, or a table laid for a meal, as a whole. Scandinavia has produced, during this century, some of the world's greater, even greatest, architects; many of them have also designed relatively small items for domestic use, and almost all have combined interior decoration in general with architecture proper. The bentwood furniture which Alvar Aalto designed in the thirties has become classically timeless, as befits the work of one who calls a chair leg 'the column's baby sister'. The Danish architect Arne Jacobsen (1901–1971) also designed furniture, some plastic and revolutionary, steel tableware and fabrics. Probably the majority of non-architect designers work in more than one, and often several media. They have a combination of restlessness and inventiveness which drives them from one medium to another and prevents the staleness inevitable in the restricted field of simple modern design. Finally, they know extremely well what they are doing. The industrial designer is frequently an artist in some respects and a practical craftsman in another. Co-operation is a native gift of the Scandinavians in many spheres, and most designers work easily as part of the whole industrial team, despite the occasional display of a prima donna attitude. The feminine, incidentally, is not ill-placed; the proportion of women among outstanding designers, though not architects, in Scandinavia is very high, especially in Finland.

One can justifiably and accurately speak of Scandinavian design as a whole, because Denmark, Finland, Norway and Sweden have developed very much on similar lines and there has been a great deal of cross-fertilization. But each country has its specialities, its fields in which it has led the others. Denmark has excelled in both metal products and furniture, and made its earliest reputation abroad through the silver of Georg Jensen, a sculptor turned silversmith. Jensen died in 1935 but had gathered round him the brilliant group of designers who have maintained and developed the Jensen style, characterized by the flowing undecorated line. Several other Danish silversmiths were profoundly influenced by Jensen, designing eventually in pewter and stainless steel as well as silver. The Danish influence was equally felt in the neighbouring Scandinavian countries, and Sweden, with its own production of high-quality steel, has had considerable success with its stainless steel tableware.

Nevertheless, it is in furniture design that Denmark has had the greatest influence on the rest of Scandinavia, and even throughout the world. Arne Jacobsen was able to tot up an impressive list of places, including some as far afield as Hawaii, Peru and Zambia, where his furniture was used in churches, hospitals, hotels, offices, town halls and universities. In Denmark, and in Copenhagen particularly, cabinet-making has a history of quality going back more than four hundred years. But the ancient Guild of Cabinet-makers has shown itself, in this century, far more interested in its future than its past. It has been instrumental in building up a collaboration with architects and designers which now extends into mass production. As has been said, the Danes pioneered the anatomically correct chair; they also saw how storage space could be increased without reducing living space. One of the earliest and still famous examples was the sideboard made by Kaare Klint in the twenties. Its starting point was an investigation of the number, shapes and sizes of pieces of glass, china, table silver and linen used in the average home. The sideboard he designed as a result was no larger than its average predecessors but held twice as much.

In the post-war years Danish furniture has run along two principal lines. The major line, now known all over the world, is the simple, modern and well-proportioned product, light and often gay in appearance, but thoroughly sound and solid as to workmanship. It has been made in a greater variety of woods than previously, and the Danes have probably been the chief influence in the rise and fall of teak. Less well known are the often exquisite adaptations, in fine mahogany, of antique furniture. These are not reproductions or copies; all superfluous decoration has been removed, leaving a piece which depends only on line, proportion and workmanship. In this the Danes have succeeded so well that many of their pieces could stand unashamedly in the same room as the eighteenth-century English furniture which has so frequently been their inspiration.

Today the chair has again become the most interesting item of Danish furniture. In the late fifties Arne Jacobsen launched his now famous 'Egg' chair, which represented an almost complete departure from chair shapes, old or new. Since then the firm of Fritz Hansen, for which Jacobsen designed, has encouraged architects of various nationalities to create new styles of chairs, most of them also breaking away from familiar lines. The eye may not always accept their shapes easily, but the body has no such difficulty. They are superlatively comfortable and basically simple. When upholstered they appear to be all of a single piece, apart from their steel or chromium legs or feet.

Finland's present field of excellence over the rest of Scandinavia is probably in textiles, although in many other forms of industrial design the Finns have recently led the rest in pure inventiveness and exuberance. The development of textiles came late. At a time when hand-weavers were already working both on yardage and purely decorative pieces, machine-made fabrics were still of a miserable over-all standard. But once individual designers began to work for the factories, the result was revolutionary. Above all, the whole attitude to colour was changed, and simple woven patterns were made dramatic by unexpected and unused combinations of colour. The same boldness characterized many printed cottons, which were the basis of Finland's earliest sallies into a type of fashion design so distinctive that it belonged to Finland and nowhere else. On the one hand the classic linen damask weave was adapted to designs never attempted before; and on the other, materials rarely before used in weaving, such as metal threads or grass, were mixed with linen or cotton. Occasionally, the mixture was more experimental than successful, but the percentage of real failures was low.

Among hand-woven pieces made by Finnish and also Norwegian and Swedish textile designers, altar cloths and ecclesiastical materials are particularly interesting. Just as Scandinavian architects of new churches have broken right away from the traditional, textile designers have created new forms and styles equally non-traditional and stimulating. They have also developed, both on a small scale for the home and a large scale for public places, wall-hangings which are the modern equivalent of the medieval tapestries of other European countries.

Norway's contribution to Scandinavian design in general is a gaiety and freshness of colour which derives from folk art, and is naturally most evident in textiles. Its more specialized craft is enamel of a type unique in the North, in decorative combinations with both silver and stainless steel. The Norwegians also produce, at the Porsgrund porcelain works, some china of great delicacy, which contrasts with the heavier, rougher cast favoured elsewhere, reflecting a certain nostalgia for the simpler pre-industrial days of a not very distant past.

The same feeling for the rough and heavy, sometimes primitive, also appears in glass in Finland, and its departure from traditional shapes and its vigorous, sometimes rugged handling have frequently made a deservedly sensational impression. But Sweden, with its longer history of glass-making, has the Scandinavian pre-eminence. Much of this position is due to its most famous glassworks, Orrefors, although there are several other long-established works of considerable standing. Swedish glass is marked by restraint, particularly when compared to Finnish, but also by the variety and perfection of its techniques. It often has a delicacy and grace less easy to find in Finland, and an elegance less common in Denmark, although the Danes, too, have produced some excellent glass.

For many years it was difficult to fault Swedish design, except on grounds of the restraint which occasionally resulted in a slightly lifeless effect. But the Swedes' recent excursions into more experimental styles and colours suggest that their gifts flower better in restraint than in revolution. Against this, their work in what might be called 'the public sector' has been highly successful. The murals by Siri Deckert on the Stockholm underground railway are an example on a large scale; the constantly redesigned telephones an example on a small scale. The important point is that Swedish industry regards it as normal to employ an artist as it does an accountant, and the benefits to the environment are bound to be considerable.

This, it seems, is the direction in which all the Scandinavian countries are likely to move. For all its brilliance and practicality, Scandinavian design has probably passed the peak of its post-war florescence, and come face to face with a variety of problems. There is a saturation point in most styles of design, and, as European homes and European taste grow increasingly standardized, the scope for variety, particularly in the simple Scandinavian style, diminishes all the time. Domestic design has gradually become for most Northern countries a staple, though not enormous, export, and the export market tends to look for novelty; only a few lines become classics, capable of indefinite repetition. The furniture industry, particularly in Denmark, is well aware of this problem. Glass and china are more obligingly perishable, and textiles subject to wear and tear. The customer wants change, which can mean opportunity; but there are also pitfalls in change for its own sake.

The worst, which has become visible in the last few years, is a deterioration in design which appears to be an overspill from pop art. This is unimportant in the trivial or ephemeral objects which, nevertheless, have now become disappointingly numerous; but it is certainly saddening to see extremely highly-priced pieces which are either non-functional by any standards or vulgar by Scandinavian standards of only a very few years ago, or both. There is an inevitable reaction against the asceticism and bloodlessness of some designs of a decade or so ago; it may be that a better equilibrium will be established after a spell which has permitted at least a small proportion of designers to throw off the restraints of functionalism and purity of line.

Another possible pitfall is the development of a disequilibrium between hand-made and machine-made goods. The Scandinavians have been admirably successful in maintaining and encouraging the best possible standards in hand-made and home-made objects, and it is rare to see anything either badly made, 'arty-crafty' in a pejorative sense, or with only limited decorative or practical value. The slogan of industrial design since the twenties has been 'More beautiful things for everyday use'; excellent as is this aim, one may wonder whether it can be carried too far when applied to the making by hand of some of the lowlier things for everyday use. Is a hand-made wooden kitchen spatula, even when designed to bring out the beauty of grain of the wood, really worth its additional cost in time and money, compared with the machine-made equivalent? Has a plain, rough towel a greater intrinsic value because it has been woven by hand?

These are instances of the reverse side of a movement which otherwise still holds plenty of scope. The redesigning of the ordinary and less ordinary implements of everyday life is a fairly constant process. Shelf paper has already been mentioned; an attack has also been made on writing paper, sometimes unfortunately so colourful that legibility could be assured only by the use of a poker dipped in tar, or some handier equivalent. More calamitous, though, on account of their *nouveau-riche* appeal, which the Scandinavians have previously rejected firmly, are the correspondence cards with envelopes lined with gold leaf, each one the price of a pound or more of butter. Pots and pans have been extensively redesigned, nearly always for the better, although male designers have occasionally overestimated the weight the average woman is capable of lifting. Scissors have been given a better line and made more comfortable to hold.

Outside the home, in theatres, schools, hotels, hospitals and institutions of all kinds, the opportunities are considerably greater. This is the field where the fresh and comprehensive eye of the Scandinavians can most profitably be used. They have, for instance, redesigned some school furniture with great savings of space and cost. They have grasped that a bedroom in a hotel requires furniture quite different from that in a bedroom in a home, and guests in some of the new hotels have experienced much greater comfort and convenience. Theatre-goers have found the new seats, where they have been installed, far more comfortable and pleasant to look at. And surgeons have benefited by a redesigned and more efficient operating table.

Another field in which the Scandinavians have excelled is display. Their exhibitions are almost always planned so that the eye is as delighted by the arrangement as a whole as by individual objects. They have also created outstanding art and exhibition galleries. Examples are found in the Henie-Onstad centre and the Munch

Museum in Oslo and in 'Louisiana', a period house north of Copenhagen which has been extended to provide a setting for contemporary exhibitions. Even the trade fairs in Helsinki are set out more attractively than most of their kind. On the other hand, the standard of displays in the windows and interiors of department and other stores is on the whole surprisingly low, and many of the larger retailers have yet to be converted to the employment of artists in display. All in all, Scandinavian designers can still find plenty of opportunities and challenges in a world bent on modernizing itself, however slowly.

But it remains less certain whether, in the foreseeable future, there will be a renaissance of the distinction of design of past years. At times the Scandinavians reached a point where the division between pure and applied art became obscured, and they were able to create objects of great beauty for their own sakes. Some of this activity is bound to continue; but it seems as though the near future for Scandinavian design will be less joyous, though no less useful, than the near past.

12   Nordic integration

SCANDINAVIA AS A WHOLE represents the most integrated group of independent states in the world. The groundwork of the Nordic community was firmly laid long before the idea of a European Economic Community was conceived. For almost a century it has been slowly, quietly and pragmatically built up. Only in the last two decades has the Nordic community been formalized and given more precise aims and institutions. It is unlike the EEC in that it has had no theoretical basis comparable to the Treaty of Rome. Instead it is the fruit of organic growth, of common patterns of daily life, and of affinities of race, language and religion. It has had its setbacks and its failures; its future shape remains indefinite. It is based on a system which is capable neither of export to nor of reproduction by other groups of countries. Yet even in its far from perfect state, it is an achievement worthy of greater note than it has generally received.

Each of the Scandinavian countries has its own distinct personality and its own particular relationship to the outside world. Nevertheless, for a long time and in many different areas of daily life the development of the five countries has been integral. Strong national feelings account in a large measure for the success of individual countries, but their strength in relation to other lands is inseparable from this integration. Though the regional personality of Scandinavia collectively is weakly defined by comparison with the personalities of its separate nations, the concept of Norden claims a growing allegiance. In the words of Stanley Anderson, Scandinavians have developed 'secondary loyalties' to complement their primary national allegiances. There are two ultimate reasons for this. Firstly, the emergence of a Scandinavian community has been and remains a form of refuge – refuge in the face of external pressures. These pressures may be cultural as well as military and commercial. Secondly, and more positively, the Scandinavian community is appreciated increasingly as a form of release – release from the restraints imposed by the somewhat narrowly drawn national boundaries. Politically, socially, economically and culturally the concept of a Scandinavian community contributes to a feeling of security.

The roots of Scandinavianism were struck five generations ago. In the first instance, they were principally intellectual and artistic, though from the outset economic arguments were voiced. The same romantic influences that fostered nationalism had their Scandinavian overtones. In part they sprang from the literary and scientific reappraisal of the Viking past. Swede, Norwegian and Dane alike began to extol the heroic qualities of their common Viking ancestors. E. Tegner's *Fritjof's Saga* (1825) and J. L. Runeberg's *King Fjalar* (1844) illustrate the point. Archeologist, linguist and historian slowly revealed a Viking achievement to set against the millennium of calumny that west Europeans had heaped upon the heads of Nordic marauders. Distinguished men of letters spoke of Iceland in the same breath as Greece. As early as 1843 a Scandinavian customs union was discussed in Danish official circles – an idea to be mooted again in the 1880s by the Danish banker C. F. Tietgen. In 1847 the first Scandinavian scientific conference was held at Roskilde.

The brotherhood of Scandinavians was widely preached in university circles. It was most demonstrative in the face of threatened assault from without. The challenge came from two different sources – Prussia in the south and Russia in the east. Denmark was invaded by Prussia in 1848 and again in 1864. Although no direct military support was given to Denmark, an immense amount of Scandinavian fervour was generated. After 1808 Sweden and Norway were never subject to direct attack by Russia, but by the late 1830s Russia was building formidable fortifications in the Åland Islands (their ruins are a tourist attraction today) and disquieting rumours of Russian infiltration into north Norway were reported regularly in dispatches sent to Lord Palmerston from Consul Crowe in Christiania (Oslo since 1924). The Crimean War (1854–56) had its side effects in the Baltic arena – not least was the formal adherence of the Grand Duchy of Finland to Russia throughout the episode. After 1856 little more was heard of Finland's lingering allegiance to Sweden, though it was not long before Finland aspired to nationhood and began to associate itself with the Scandinavian community in its own right.

It was matters social – not political or economic – that prompted the first practical steps taken towards Scandinavianism. The lawyers led the way in 1872 with a meeting of Scandinavian jurists (and they still maintain the century-old tradition). The first Scandinavian labour congress, held in 1886, had an eye on social security, but it was twenty years before Denmark, Norway and Sweden initiated discussions on state accident insurance. Since Finland participated in 1919 and Iceland in 1946 the regular discussions have now broadened into general insurance congresses. To the same year (1907) as the discussions on insurance belongs the foundation of the Scandinavian Inter-Parliamentary Union, to be joined by Finland and Iceland after the First World War. In 1919 there came into being the Norden Association, the avowed aim of which was to promote Scandinavian co-operation and understanding in the fullest possible manner. Since then, a unique and tensile web of political, social, technical and commercial threads has been woven. It shows that if Scandinavianism is functional in purpose it is popular in expression.

The popular expression of Scandinavianism is witnessed in the network of day-to-day contacts across the entire spectrum of society. At government level, the foreign ministers of the five countries meet twice annually, the ministers of social welfare and education biennially. All professions and vocations have their Scandinavian as well as their national expressions – from tanners and brewers, through farmers and foresters, missionaries and post office managers, doctors and dentists, to the directors of central banks and prison officers. Beyond this, the Scandinavians are as avid in their conventioneering as the Americans. Meetings can take most varied forms, from specialized research seminars for high-powered representatives to simple annual gatherings of the heads of specialist libraries to standardize procedures, from the assemblies of university rectors to meetings of farmers' organizations (from, for example, the Swedish and Finnish sides of the Torni valley) or of fishery inspectors whose provinces are the common freshwater boundaries of Lapland.

Educationally the Nordic countries operate increasingly as one. At the university (including the technical and commercial university) level the examinations taken in one country are recognized as equivalent for all institutions of higher learning throughout Scandinavia. Scholarships and student loans are available for the interchange of students. There is also interavailability of bursaries for students between the folk high schools. Intra-Nordic university research projects help specialist centres to cater for the needs of all five countries and to eliminate the need for duplication of facilities in each country. There is, for example, a Nordic school of public health in Gothenburg. For appointments to senior academic posts, advice is sought from experts in universities across the five countries. For the schools, there is co-operation in the publication of textbooks which present an agreed Scandinavian interpretation of facts and events.

In another major field of communication, radio and television, the Scandinavians experience problems common to all small countries with restricted revenues. In addition Norway and Iceland suffer difficulties for purely topographical reasons. Not surprisingly there has been long and widespread co-operation in this field. A common Nordic television market is declared a reality. Language affinity (Finland apart) enables many programmes to enjoy a Scandinavian currency. On the one hand, the range of available talent is greatly increased through co-operation. On the other, such programmes as television theatre, operating over Nordvision, can entertain audiences of millions. In the associated musical sphere there is a Nordic Union of Musicians and common protection of performing rights for composers.

Twinning arrangements between towns and the interchange of local government officials and club members have a fuller meaning for Scandinavians than elsewhere, because they have been broadened into a system of Friendship Towns. This system, which embraces towns from each of four, if not five, countries, seeks to broaden the range of family and workshop contacts at least as much as to promote official connections. Nor have the Lapps been left out of the common deliberations. Regular meetings of Lappologists are held in the North not only for the exchange of academic information, but also with a view to protecting increasingly vulnerable territory. The intrusion of industry and tourism upon the traditional reindeer territories with its consequent erosion of their distinctive cultural features has given rise to a co-ordinated resistance movement between Finland, Norway and Sweden.

Against the background of experience built up through the annual gatherings of the Nordic Inter-Parliamentary Union and of confidence created through these manifold social and personal connections, the governments of the Scandinavian countries moved towards the establishment of fuller consultative organizations. Although an inter-Scandinavian cabinet conference in 1949 sought unsuccessfully to create a military alliance between Denmark, Norway and Sweden, the discussions nevertheless opened the way to proposals for the creation of a Nordic Council. In 1952 the parliaments of Denmark, Iceland, Norway and Sweden formally approved the proposals and the Council met for the first time in 1953. It has met annually since that year, with Finland joining as a full member in 1955 and attending the Copenhagen session for the first time in 1956. In 1957 the Council met in Helsinki. The Lapps have no independent representation in the Nordic Council, but the Faeroese and Ålanders keep a watching brief.

The Nordic Council has no headquarters, but assembles in a different Scandinavian capital each year. It has 69 elected members – sixteen each from Denmark, Finland, Norway and Sweden, and five from Iceland. Members are elected from the parliaments of the five countries with a system of representation proportional to the strength of their political parties. Depending upon matters for discussion, a number of non-voting cabinet ministers also attend – in practice between twenty and thirty. An elected Presidium, consisting of a President and four Vice-Presidents, continues the work of the Council between its annual meetings. Each national delegation has its own secretariat. Four permanent committees cover the judiciary, social policy, economic matters and cultural affairs. With its general absence of bureaucratic restraint and its flexibility of operation, the Council has provided a setting in which the enterprise and energy of individuals can be exercised to the full. Some measure of the success of the Nordic Council is contained in an observation by the Swedish politician Bertil Ohlin. During the Council's first thirteen sessions 250 recommendations were adopted and the governments concerned followed up with positive action all but a fifth of them.

Examples of proposals which have come before the Council, have been supported by all of the Scandinavian parliaments and have given rise to organizations in their own right are research institutions for theoretical physics (Nordita, as it is called) and maritime law, a Nordic Board of Marine Biology and graduate institutes for press research, hygiene and domestic science. More recently a top-level council for applied research (Nordforsk) has been created. Although cultural co-operation is in any case strong, it has been given a significant boost through the establishment of a Nordic Cultural Fund. A Nordic Council for the Fine Arts advises the officers of the fund, while assessment of original works of art at a Scandinavian level emerges through Nordic prizes for literature and music.

Although a Joint Nordic Committee for Economic Co-operation had sprung into being in 1948 and submitted a report on the widespread advantages to be gained from broadening the basis of economic activity, it was not until 1954–55 that members of the Nordic Council began to debate seriously the practical possibilities of a Nordic Common Market. By this time Finland was entering the fold of the Nordic Council and had expressed favourable reactions to the proposals. Russian pressures, already manifest at the time of Finland's association with the Council, were reiterated. Nevertheless, a five-volume report emerged from the Council in 1957 and adoption of its recommendations was virtually unanimous.

Already before the Council had come into existence Denmark, Finland, Norway and Sweden had organized a common passport area for their citizens. They were joined by Iceland in 1955. Given this background and the goodwill of the trade unions, it was possible to contemplate a common labour market. Although it was not until 1954 that Denmark, Finland, Norway and Sweden signed the convention that dispensed with work permits in each other's countries, intra-Scandinavian labour exchanges had been in existence for nine years. During the years of post-war reconstruction Norway and Finland had been reluctant to encourage a free flow of their much-needed labour force to Sweden. In any case, they were losing a fair amount of skilled labour overseas and the shadow of a brain drain lay over them. Despite the differential attractions of the five countries for each other's work forces, labour migration was modest during the first ten years of the common labour market. But as economic decline showed on the horizon, as the proportionately stronger position of the Swedish *krona* became clear, and as confidence in moving beyond the frontiers of the homeland grew, migration into Sweden from the neighbouring Scandinavian lands gathered momentum. The movement reached a peak during 1969–70. By then there were many scores of thousands of Scandinavians working in Nordic countries other than their parent lands. Such mobility has been a stimulus to ideas at all levels. Needless to say, it has resulted in a large number of inter-Scandinavian marriages. A Canadian author once defined the exchange of population between the USA and Canada as the greatest reciprocity movement in history. Within its narrower limits interchange of peoples has produced a similar situation in Scandinavia.

The effects have been the most significant for the Finns, who are ethnographically the least Scandinavian and at the same time have proved the most mobile of the Nordic peoples in recent years. In 1970 alone there was a balance of emigrants to Sweden approximating to 45,000 – a figure equalling one per cent of the total Finnish population and exceeding the maximum number of Finns who were moving to the New World for any year during the great age of emigration at the beginning of the century. By 1970, too, there were an estimated 250,000 citizens of Finnish origin resident in Sweden. One of the problems has been the highly selective character of the emigration. In 1970 forty per cent of the Finnish emigrants to Sweden were from Lapland and Oulu counties – and only 13 per cent of Finland's population lives here. A Finnish government commission has been established to consider why (to use the words of a current publication) there should be so many 'refugees from the homeland' – the more so in that the movement has contributed substantially to a decline in the total population of Finland for the first time in many decades. Nor is the situation in the host country without embarrassment. The Finns form a sufficiently large minority to form a pressure group in their own right. Among other facilities, the Ministry of Education in Sweden has been asked to provide special Finnish-language teaching in schools.

The integration of the Scandinavian countries was given a new twist in 1959. The principal market for all of them was Britain – and Britain had a substantially negative balance of trade with Scandinavia collectively. In the context of the Continent, Britain sought to create an alternative marketing area to the European Economic Community. This took the form of the European Free Trade Area which came into being in Stockholm in July 1959. An immediate consequence was that Finland, which by 1959 had expressed willingness to join a Nordic Common Market, found itself outside a commercial agreement which centred upon its principal customer. Largely because Russian misgivings were expressed over EFTA, it took more than two years for Finland to find a solution to the problem. In any case, Finland could neither contract out of its most-favoured-nation arrangement with the USSR nor jeopardize its bilateral trading agreements with the countries of eastern Europe. A compromise of Gilbertian ingenuity was reached. In the words of Finland's ambassador to the United Nations, Max Jakobson, 'Finland did not join EFTA. Instead, EFTA joined it.' Or to put it another way, a separate free trade area was created to accommodate the political needs of Finland, whereby Finland became an associate member of EFTA. Iceland was the last of the Scandinavian countries to join EFTA, in 1970.

EFTA not only generated greatly increased trade between the United Kingdom and Scandinavia; it radically altered the pattern of trading between the Scandinavian countries themselves. For example, Sweden became Denmark's second export market, its principal market for manufactured goods, Finland's second most important source of imports after West Germany. EFTA also stimulated development because of its financial promotion. In the decade following 1961, for example, about threequarters of the foreign investment in Finland derived from EFTA sources. This included British loans for the development of the Rautaruukki steel plant and Swedish investment in car assembly works (partly to profit from cheaper Finnish labour). Nevertheless, it is an interesting reflection that when Finland purchased its first atomic energy plant it was obtained from the USSR, in spite of the more competitive rates offered by EFTA partners.

Schemes for a common Nordic market were put into cold storage with the establishment of EFTA, though the Association imposed no restraints upon special trading arrangements within its framework. Successful though EFTA was to prove, the Scandinavians have been continuously mindful of the greater economic potential of EEC. Denmark applied for membership in 1961, Norway in 1967. Despite keen interest on the part of her industrialists, Sweden maintained a detached position. It was the initiative of Denmark that set in motion plans for a Nordic Economic Union in the late 1960s. This was immediately christened Nordek and in 1970 the Nordic Council put forward proposals that it should be ratified by the governments of Denmark, Finland, Norway and Sweden. Theoretically, Nordek could contribute much to the strength of Scandinavia's position, but throughout the debates on it, there was an undercurrent of opposition. Once again the sensitivity of Finland was evident, despite built-in clauses to accommodate a variety of situations. Perhaps the most important of these clauses stated that if a member of Nordek wished to enter EEC any other member had the right to apply for its own suspension from Nordek until all four countries were agreed upon the consequent adjustments required in their own union. In the event, largely owing to Finland's difficult situation, ratification of the Nordek proposals proved impossible.

Nordek contained a number of imaginative ideas. In addition to the long-discussed customs union, it planned the establishment of a central Scandinavian financial institution consisting of an investment bank, an agriculture fund, a fisheries fund and a general purposes fund. Income for the institution was to to be derived from a levy proportionate to the gross national product of the participating countries – Sweden contributing a maximum of 45 per cent, Finland a minimum of 10 per cent. The principal purpose of the institution was to stimulate a freer flow of capital throughout Scandinavia, in place of the present restricted movement, with the intention of strengthening weaker sections of the economy and of assisting the underdeveloped areas.

Nordic commercial co-operation will intensify regardless of the failure of Nordek to come into being. Standardization and rationalization are keynotes of its development. Both processes appeal to the old-established Scandinavian consumer and producer co-operatives, the very magnitude of whose dealings enable them to effect economies in intra-Scandinavian trade. Their own special journal *Nordkoop* looks in particular to co-operation in the productive process and in the bulk purchase of specialized products. The interchange of processing techniques, the standardization of legal practices (such as the registration and protection of patents), and the standardization of information systems (from the collection and publication of statistics to the methods of analysis of foodstuffs) illustrated a deepening realization of functional co-operation. In a sense, the Nordic Postal Union led the way in 1934, with the adoption of standard practices over the whole spectrum of Scandinavia's postal services.

Rationalization has been proceeding quietly and effectively at the Scandinavian level in a number of areas. For example, between 1953 and 1968 over ninety agreements were made with this aim in view, while a regular publication on *Scandinavian Mergers and Acquisitions* is devoted to structural rationalization. Among the best-known leaders in this direction have been Scandinavia's aviation services.

The cost of operating a fleet of international passenger aircraft is daunting for a small country, though Finland and Iceland operate limited international services with success. But of a different stature is Scandinavian Airline Services (SAS) which came into existence in 1946. SAS operates a world-wide network and has pioneered many new routes, best-known of which are the trans-polar routes to the west coast of North America and East Asia, which were started in 1954.

Transport is central to other experiments in rationalization. A shipping consortium was established in Gothenburg in 1967 with a view to co-ordinating container and unit cargo traffic. In this context, a committee of the Nordic Council has put forward wide-ranging proposals for treating Scandinavia's transport systems as unitary from the standpoint of international trading. Gothenburg is regarded as a possible point of assembly for large-scale ocean traffic, while Copenhagen is its prospective complement for Nordic long-distance air freight. It is realized that a common oil harbour for Scandinavia could make for major economies, though the existing heavy investment in national oil harbours and refineries militates against it. Technical co-operation in the exploitation of North Sea gas and oil will doubtless occur.

It is not surprising that, against the background of the ever-increasing demand for energy, there should be concern over the rationalization of power supplies. A Nordic Electricity Committee (Nordel) now aims at the co-ordination of water power, oil and (prospectively) natural gas supplies. Although there are local and regional exchanges of energy, for example between the Swedish and Danish sides of the Sound, between the Swedish and Finnish sides of Torni river, and between Sweden and Norway in the hinterland of Trondheim, there is no inter-Scandinavian grid system. There are still major economies to be made in the production and distribution of energy, remembering among other facts the different time zone in which Finland operates. An immediate objective of Nordel is the production of a 15 per cent effective reserve of energy common to Denmark, Norway and Sweden.

The common borderlands of the Scandinavian countries, indeed, offer special possibilities of fruitful co-operation. In the neglected sub-Arctic territories of Finland, Norway and Sweden, it is increasingly realized that problems can be better approached collectively than separately. In Nordkalotten, at the meeting ground of the three countries, there is increasing co-operation at large and in detail to deal with the social and economic problems that spring from its extensive areas, occupied by a thin scatter of people in a harsh climate. In detail, there is co-operation in health services across the borders and, in some places, there are common schools. Communications are treated unitarily and there is a vigorous promotion of the tourist trade – not least in the encouragement to use Nordkalotten for inter-Scandinavian conferences.

There is a second and completely contrasting Scandinavian area where common planning is pursued with growing enthusiasm. The Öresund region, shared by Denmark and Sweden, has the most rapidly increasing population in Scandinavia. It is forecast that by the year 2000 its present 2.6 million inhabitants will have swollen to at least four millions. This is the most favoured area of Scandinavia both physically and in relation to the Continent. Planning for its fuller integration includes a new airport on the island of Saltholm, with tunnels and bridges across the Sound to both Sweden and Denmark. The complex urban area of Copenhagen-Malmö bears comparison with that of Rotterdam-Antwerp in the Benelux setting. Not surprisingly such a large potential population concentration offers other challenges. The Scandinavians are generally alert to the problems of water pollution – particularly of sewage and industrial waste entering the virtually tideless Baltic and the sluggish waters of its approaches. Again, a committee of the Nordic Council has undertaken a survey of what is sometimes called the Scandinavian Sea (Kattegat, the Sound, Skagerrak). Dr Stockmann, the medical officer of health in Ibsen's *An Enemy of the People*, would have gloated over its findings. All the cities and towns around the Scandinavian Sea are to a greater or lesser extent responsible for issuing untreated sewage into the sea. The committee, which has been bold enough to expose the problem and to urge a collective approach to its solution, has cast its eyes west to the North Sea and east to the Baltic. The Nordic Council hopes that the North Sea states will follow its own example and that collective action may prevent the enclosed Baltic from becoming a dead sea.

As in EEC, major problems are posed in Scandinavia by agriculture and fishing. These problems relate both to Nordic integration and to the possible entry into EEC of one or more of the Northern countries. To take agriculture first, the costs of farm production differ greatly between the Scandinavian countries. Within the framework of EFTA, problems are minimal; on entry into EEC, they would be fundamental. Though otherwise united, Scandinavia is divided over entry on the score of its established agricultural policies. Production costs of Danish agriculture, which operates without subsidies, are substantially below the average costs of the EEC countries. For the other Scandinavian lands, production costs exceed those of the EEC group, and vary from 5 per cent more for Sweden to 15 per cent more for Norway and Finland. And in all these countries farming is supported both directly and indirectly. A unitary price level for farm products throughout Scandinavia would be difficult to achieve. There are other factors which complicate the intra-Scandinavian agricultural situation. Firstly, farming is important in many parts for the effective functioning of society independently of the efficient operation of the economy. Secondly, it is cheaper for Finland, Iceland and Norway to import grain and raw sugar from the New World than to absorb any Danish or Swedish surpluses. Moreover, grain imports are usually written into Finland's long-term trade agreements with the USSR. Thirdly, thanks to biological and technological improvements there are substantial surpluses of farm products, especially in Denmark, Sweden and Finland. Production has run ahead of consumption in those commodities for which the Northern lands are physically suited.

Sweden has taken the lead in correcting this situation. It expects to have reduced its cultivated area by 1 to 1½ million hectares by 1980. In 1969 Finland introduced radical legislation which aims at cutting down fodder and milk production, especially in the areas of low productivity in the north. Its programme is planned to last five years, with an annual reduction of 90,000 hectares of farm land and 40,000 dairy cattle. In the immediate future, the scheme bears resemblance to the American Soil Bank; in the longer term, afforestation of at least some of the land can be expected. While the demand for farm products stagnates, that for softwood timber expands increasingly. In any future association of Scandinavia with EEC, comparative costs would strongly favour a timber crop over farm crops in Finland, Norway and Sweden.

In the fishing industry it is Iceland and Norway who would be the most likely to suffer unless their interests were protected on entry into EEC. To expose Icelandic fisheries to the operations of the Common Market countries would be a national disaster. Even Norway's diversified economy would find difficulty in absorbing the impact that competition from the fishermen of mainland Europe would have on the fortunes of the 32,000 men who look exclusively to fishing for a living (and of another 12,000 who regard it as a part-time pursuit). The co-operative sales organization, with its monopolistic features, is also a stumbling block to Norway's entry into the Common Market. Certainly the redefinition of boundaries at sea is implicit in Scandinavian association with EEC.

The integration of the Scandinavian community may be interpreted in a number of ways. Negatively, it might be regarded as the product of compulsive gregariousness rooted in a Strindbergian claustrophobia. Positively, it may be viewed as providing a structure in which the particular talents of the individual countries are increasingly a function of the group as a whole. Because of this integration, the Nordic countries are able to absorb if not resolve the problems that spring from a divided Europe, though a divided Europe must always imply to a certain extent a divided Scandinavia. EFTA has given much to the Scandinavian community – not least in helping its members to prepare for entry into a wider European community. For many reasons, despite their unity, the Scandinavians must necessarily approach EEC as individual countries. There can be no package deal for entry; rather a series of formulae will have to be devised to accommodate each country. Iceland and Norway are highly sensitive about their coastal waters. Finland is inevitably a problem country, and the Finnish President has declared: 'We have never considered, and never shall consider, membership of, or association with the EEC.' Instead Finland seeks some form of commercial arrangement with the countries of both western and eastern Europe. EEC has political overtones which have not been heard in EFTA. EFTA aimed ultimately at a free trade area for industrial goods. In 1970 the Deputy Secretary-General of EFTA, a Swede, stated: 'EFTA is not a customs union; still less a future economic union; least of all a political union in embryo.' This is the kind of body that many Scandinavians have come to appreciate. EEC is a much more strongly centralized organization differing greatly from the loose structure of EFTA. With their experiences in the relaxed and unbureaucratic Nordic Council, the Scandinavians have natural anxieties about the cost benefits of membership of or association with the European Community.

Meanwhile, Scandinavia's remarkable economic and social progress during the last generation remains indisputable. 'The golden sixties' is the phrase employed by Norway to describe the degree of its development during the last decade. To this development EFTA has made an important contribution. Over and above this, the consequences of Nordic co-operation and integration have been progressive and impressive. Efficiency, economy and competition have all been stimulated, while in social and educational fields the pooling of ideas and resources has led to better facilities at less cost. Hand in hand with economic co-operation has developed an ever-widening co-operation on cultural, social and personal levels. These are benefits which the Scandinavians know cannot be conferred, in the near future at least, by membership of the European Community.

13 Scandinavia and the world

SCANDINAVIA HAS PROVIDED European history with a prime example of national and regional *volte-face*. It has shown the extent to which national characteristics, and the actions they inspire, can change. Today the Scandinavian countries rarely figure in the headlines of the world's newspapers. A thousand years ago the Vikings were carrying news, mostly unwanted, of their homelands westward to Normandy, Britain, the Faeroes, Iceland, Greenland, even America; southward to Spain and the Mediterranean; and eastward through Russia to Constantinople. Only three hundred years ago the Swedish kings were pursuing an aggressive military policy, while in this century, Sweden has been anxious and able to avoid involvement in two world wars. Today Scandinavia is seen as a point of peace and stability in a world of conflict; a thousand years ago men all over Europe were echoing, in their different tongues and different forms, the prayer, 'From the fury of the Norsemen, good Lord deliver us.'

It was not all fury, but it was a colonial activity more wide-reaching than that of Rome. The Scandinavian countries of Viking times were semi-tribal societies, lacking either central governments or established monarchies. With either of these they might have become the first imperial power to hold at least temporary sway over an empire beyond the ocean. Instead their colonization was fragmentary, often short-lived, and left relatively few permanent marks. To England, however, they brought some of their own legal practices, among them the jury system. Today one third of the peoples of the world have legal systems based on English law. So, paradoxically, at least a small element of the civilizing influence of the law has been derived from the raids of the Vikings. Nevertheless, the Vikings probably took back to their homelands more than they gave. As a result of their excursions they certainly introduced elements of European culture to Scandinavia, most important among them the beginnings of Christianity.

Thus the next time that these Northern peoples were to make their impact on Europe was as champions of Protestantism under the leadership of the Swedish king Gustavus Adolphus, in the Thirty Years' War. Lutheranism spread more quickly and struck deeper roots in Scandinavia than in any other part of the world, not excluding the German lands. Conversion to the Lutheran faith was a major turning point in Scandinavian development. Its almost total adoption made the Nordic countries as homogeneous in religion as were the Catholic strongholds of Italy and Spain. Today, although individual adherence is often more nominal than real, the Scandinavian churches are regarded as the theological leaders in world Lutheranism; and at home churchmen have a status and influence more powerful than in most countries. Even so, a residual fear of Catholicism is often as deeply-entrenched in non-believers as in practising Lutherans.

The Lutheran philosophy eventually helped to convert Scandinavia's general indigence into a widely shared prosperity. The nineteenth century reduced the fortunes of all the Northern countries to a low ebb, and poverty and famine seemed to bite more deeply than ever. The Lutheran emphasis on education and self-help partly enabled the Scandinavians to lift themselves, if slowly, out of their economic difficulties. They were also aided by their increasingly liberal attitude to foreign merchants and entrepreneurs. Already Netherlanders, Germans and Scots had established industries and dynasties among them. The Scots gave to Finland a Ramsay, one of whose descendants became Finnish Prime Minister; to Sweden a clan of von Fersens who were Macphersons when they first arrived; to Norway a Greig who left his homeland after the Battle of Culloden and whose grandson, Edvard Grieg, was to be the most Norwegian of Norway's composers.

Immigration of this type could neither prevent nor compensate for the mass emigration and escape from famine and unemployment resulting partly from a rapid population increase. By 1900 there were in the United States more than a million men and women who had been born in Scandinavia; that is, the equivalent of more than ten per cent of the total population living in Scandinavia in the same year. These emigrants were for the most part drawn to the lakes and forests of the upper Middle West. Until about 1920, when mass emigration from the Northern countries came to an end, the Scandinavians were welcomed in the States for their industry, literacy, adaptability and loyalty. The contribution of the emigrants to the development of the modern USA was, in fact, Scandinavia's first real gift in the interchange between nations. Since 1950 Scandinavia has shared with the rest of Europe the newer form of emigration to North America – the brain drain. In the years 1955–61 Norway provided a higher proportion – 16 per cent – of its total output of scientists and engineers than any other European country except Switzerland, with 17 per cent. The percentages of the United Kingdom and Sweden were 7.4 and 8.8 respectively.

From nineteenth-century Scandinavia there came the powerful stimulus of a group of highly original figures in the world of the arts. The stir they created in the intellectual placidity of the Pax Victoriana was at times almost comparable to the fury of the Norsemen. The greatest impact was made by the drama. By the turn of the century several of Henrik Ibsen's plays had been seen in Berlin, Paris and London, where *Ghosts* scandalized critics and public alike in 1891. Meanwhile, in the early nineties, Berliners were seeing the first performances in German of Strindberg's plays. Both dramatists were vortices about whom men and ideas whirled. Not least among those drawn into their system was the Norwegian artist Edvard Munch. In the early nineteen hundreds audiences in London and Berlin began to hear in the works of Jean Sibelius a new and original kind of music. These four great figures alone were able to prove that the then remote North had its own distinctive offering to make to European culture. The interest of a wider public was aroused by the exploits of the Norwegian explorers Fridtjof Nansen and Roald Amundsen, whose lineal descendant of our own times is Thor Heyerdahl. Gradually, over this century, the North has extended its interest and its influence into many other spheres – social, technological, economic and political. Relative to their size, the Scandinavian countries today play as great a part in world affairs as any other fully-developed nations.

More than that, Scandinavia now exerts its own influence in spheres where it was formerly subjected to influences from outside. The character of its relationship to the rest of the world, as well as its dimensions, has changed. When the tsars who succeeded Peter the Great were bent on giving St Petersburg the proportions of greatness they sought their principal architect, Bartolomeo Rastrelli, in Italy.

When Alexander I set about rebuilding Helsinki as a capital he entrusted the work to a German, C. L. Engel. Today any country in search of an architect of distinction is likely to turn to Scandinavia, and especially to Finland. Eliel Saarinen influenced the design of the American skyscraper, Wiljö Rewell gave Toronto its City Hall; the Dane Arne Jacobsen was the architect of St Catherine's College, Oxford; Alvar Aalto has designed for many other countries, among them the USA, Germany and even Italy – a reversal of the practice of former days, when Italy so often provided inspiration for buildings, if not also their architects. And in the lesser, but more pervasive form of applied art, domestic and industrial design, the words 'Scandinavian design' have become as overworked as its products have been imitated. At a lower level the Northern countries have had a world influence on eating habits. From the breakfast table they have advanced at least to the luncheon table. Rye bread, crisp bread, lager and akvavit are accompaniments to the *smörgåsbord* – now, like Scandinavian design, reproduced or imitated in many parts of the world. Yet the lapse of time since the days when for the Scandinavians even rice was a luxury import, can still be measured in decades.

In spite of their more generalized impact on the outside world, food, drink and design are little more than the small change of a far greater development in international trade. Scandinavia started with considerable supplies of three commodities in world demand – fish, softwoods and iron ore. To these it added eventually the high technical expertise of its citizens, thus enabling the export of large-scale capital goods, together with assistance in their installation and operation. Increasingly, the Scandinavians are becoming engineers to the world. Naturally the volume of their operations is relatively limited. Nevertheless, together with the United Kingdom and Japan, Sweden is one of the world's leading shipbuilders. Some of Sweden's largest firms have international ramifications and subsidiary plants abroad – among them SKF (ball- and roller-bearings), L. M. Ericsson (telecommunications equipment), Atlas-Copco (compressed air equipment), and Electrolux. A part of the success of the Scandinavian countries springs from their concentration on industrial production related to their own experience and environment. Thus Finland can now claim the world's most advanced icebreaker laboratory, jointly sponsored by Esso and Wärtsilä. Out of its experience with native clay and chalk, Denmark has become a major producer of complete plants for the cement industry (it has sold them to eighty different countries), a specialist in cements for hot and cold climates, a builder of bridges, harbours and cooling towers for a world market. Against the background of animal husbandry, Denmark also produces complete meat processing plants for export; while Norway's concern with fishing has stimulated an export trade in fish-processing factories.

Export operations on this scale are unusual in countries small in population and generally classified as young industrially. Even the Finns, with a significant engineering industry dating back only to 1944, now construct and export at least twelve per cent of the world's paper-making machines. Engineers on temporary appointments install them as far afield as South-east Asia and Latin America. Finns have also constructed entire softwood factory complexes in Rumania and the USSR and their success has gained them orders for Siberian installations. The speed with which the Northern countries have developed these world-wide connections is partly explained by their experience in the paper and pulp industry. Softwood products, basic to the foreign trade of Finland, Norway and Sweden, can be economically and efficiently produced only on a large scale, with a far bigger export than home market, and a constant renewal of equipment and techniques. Countries forced to operate in these conditions, however young they may be industrially, have acquired the habit of thinking more comprehensively and applying the experience gained in one field to the development of another.

Towards the international flow of capital the Scandinavian countries have varying policies. All import capital, but with reservations. All are jealous of foreign ownership. Iceland will not establish its own oil refinery unless more than half the shares are owned by Icelanders. The Danes have legislation to restrict the German purchase of summer homes along their coasts. Foreign investment in Finland is inseparable from the most-favoured-nation treatment that it enjoys with the USSR and the corresponding potential of the Russian market for Finnish goods. No Scandinavian country will permit foreign ownership unless it is clearly beneficial to its own economy. However, the problem, common to several Western European countries, of how much American investment is beneficial has barely touched the Nordic area. American firms are less interested in operating in the relatively small Scandinavian market than in gaining a foothold inside the tariff walls of the far larger European Economic

Community. All the Scandinavian countries except Iceland invest abroad. The softwood industries of Canada are particularly favoured. Within Scandinavia, Sweden has an active investment policy, especially in Finland.

The most searching and still partly unresolved problem of the post-war years has been the role which each country of the North is to play on the world political stage. Before the Second World War the Scandinavian countries had virtually no policies beyond the avoidance of entanglements. Yet as long ago as the First World War Rudolf Kjellén, a political scientist at Gothenburg School of Economics, had characterized Sweden, and by inference Scandinavia, as an area especially sensitive to the strains and stresses that develop between more broadly based land power and sea power. He held that the great powers could be divided into those of military and those of economic origin. The former, Kjellén believed, were the product of a continental environment which encouraged military activity and political discipline: the latter, born of a maritime environment, were stimulated to liberalism by movement across the seas and the need to exchange. The Scandinavian countries were sensitive jointly to the military power of the Baltic rim and economic power of the Atlantic front. They might rejoice in a northern detachment from the pivotal areas of mainland Europe, but they could only enjoy security when there was an effective equilibrium between Germany and Russia, the United Kingdom and by implication the USA. A generation later, a study group of the Royal Institute of International Affairs expressed the situation in another way: 'The geographical position of these nations has placed them during recent decades in a sort of political vacuum preserved by counterbalancing pressures.'

All the Scandinavian countries have sought an escape from these pressures in neutrality. It served them well enough in the First World War; but during the inter-war years escape became escapism, a near-blind belief that the mere word 'neutrality' was sufficient to deter the aggressor. Yet neutrality, whether a form of escape or escapism, did and still does correspond to an important element in the Northern temperament. Thus even today the attitude adopted by each country vis-à-vis the world is one of compromise in commitment or in neutrality. Denmark and Norway, though members of NATO, will not allow American bases on their soil. Iceland, also part of NATO, finds its new strategic situation disturbing. Sweden and Finland have taken up, in place of this modified commitment, positions of modified neutrality. Sweden, by free choice, has given preference to non-alignment. Finland, without choice, has had to adjust its neutrality to suit the Soviet Union.

The Northern countries were taken largely by surprise, in the Second World War, by the Soviet attack on Finland and the German invasion of Denmark and Norway. They were confused by the Soviet-Finnish settlement which appeared to remove Finland from the Scandinavian political orbit, and they realized during the ensuing cold war that the formulation of a more definite policy had become inescapable. At first Denmark, Norway and Sweden considered the formation of a neutral bloc. Bent on dividing the North, the Soviet Union expressed disapproval of what it regarded as an anti-Soviet military plot. The divisive aims of the USSR succeeded, and the North split neatly into Atlantic and Baltic Scandinavia. Sweden, looking warily eastwards, was preoccupied by 'the Finnish question'. In Stockholm the view was generally held that closer alignment with pro-Anglo-Saxon Denmark and Norway would cause the Soviet Union to tighten its hold over Finland. The Iron Curtain would then be drawn through the Gulf of Bothnia, far too close to Sweden for comfort. By 1949 the Northern countries had settled into the positions they hold today. Denmark and Norway, dominated by their experience in Hitler's War, feared being again cut off from immediate aid. Together with Iceland they joined NATO. Sweden opted to maintain the neutrality which had already lasted since 1815. Finland concluded in 1948 an Agreement on Friendship, Co-operation and Mutual Assistance with the USSR, which confirmed and developed the special form of neutrality already enforced by the Peace Treaty.

Retrospectively, and in the general European context, the differing neutralities of Sweden and Finland provide unusual examples of the interplay of both internal and external pressures. The general European conception of neutrality derives from Switzerland, whose special form of non-commitment has been internationally guaranteed since 1815. The world would be shocked, or at least surprised, to hear the Swiss president or a government representative make any provocative pronouncement on international affairs. It expects Switzerland to provide a neutral location for international organizations, to mind its own business in peace-time, and to look after the diplomatic business of belligerents in times of conflict. It is neutrality at its most classic. If Switzerland did not exist, it would have been necessary to invent it. Whether Europe could contain or make use of more than one Switzerland is a matter for academic debate. Sweden and Finland were neither politically nor psychologically in positions to emulate the Swiss stance, and in the post-war decades, both have evolved their own conceptions of the neutral way.

Finland is an example of the unnatural neutral – a country whose people, individually and collectively, have strong passions and prejudices, loves and hates. The fence is no place for them to sit, yet they have contrived to sit on it fairly comfortably, while putting their greater weight on its western side. The most important provisions of the Agreement on Co-operation and Mutual Assistance with the Soviet Union obliged Finland to repel any attack made on Russia through Finland by Germany and her allies; and to confer with the Soviet Union if such an attack seemed to threaten. Unlike the treaties made by the Soviet Union with Rumania, Hungary and Czechoslovakia, the agreement with Finland did not demand a general subordination of foreign policy to the Kremlin. Nor was Finland expected to take part in the Warsaw Pact when it was signed in 1955 as an eastern riposte to the admission of West Germany to NATO.

Every Finnish president since the war – Mannerheim, Paasikivi and Kekkonen – and the Finnish people themselves have grasped clearly that the country's future depended first and foremost on the establishment of a good-neighbour policy towards the USSR. Juho Paasikivi, president from 1946 to 1956, was the real architect of this policy. Under him it succeeded so well, and led to such a considerable relaxation of tension that in 1955 Finland was able to become a member both of the United Nations and the Nordic Council; equally significant, in the same year the USSR dismantled its 900-square-mile military base at Porkkala, west of Helsinki, and returned it to Finland. Thus when President Kekkonen assumed office in 1956 he inherited a solid foundation on which to build his own form of neutrality. Though remaining as mindful as ever of Paasikivi's maxim, 'Never cross the Soviet path', Kekkonen has not had to carry the weight of history that hung on his predecessor. He has therefore been able to combine neutrality with greater activity and initiative than was possible in the early post-war years.

Finland's foreign policy under Kekkonen has developed along two main lines: first, co-operation within the framework of the United Nations, to be discussed later in this chapter; second, extension beyond Sweden of a neutral North to take in Denmark, Iceland and Norway, despite their commitment to NATO. In the latter context, the Kalott area, where Norway and Finland march with the USSR, is especially sensitive. In this area – specifically along the Pasvik river – NATO and the Warsaw Pact organization face each other. Both Sweden and Finland have seen this situation as a potential source of trouble. Indeed, at one point in the sixties, panic followed the Pentagon's calculations that missiles launched from the Soviet side of the Kalott area could be delivered neatly, by way of the North Pole, on certain cities of North America. President Kekkonen's reaction was to suggest a treaty between Finland and Norway to safeguard and possibly de-militarize the Kalott, but it received no favourable response from Norway. Nor have his repeated proposals to create a formal nuclear-free Scandinavian zone been any more successful. Both Denmark and Norway have refused to admit American bases on their territory and therefore regard a nuclear-free zone as *de facto* existing. Kekkonen, however, considers this as insufficient, and wishes to see such a zone given a *de jure* basis, possibly involving a modification of Norway's position within NATO.

By virtue of the ultimate responsibility for foreign affairs conferred by his office the Finnish president is peculiarly vulnerable to criticism. Inside and outside Finland Kekkonen has been criticized on the grounds that he has gone further than is necessary in his friendship with the Soviet Union and that, by extension, he pursues a policy inspired by the USSR. There is no evidence to confirm or refute this criticism. But it is certain that, had the creation of a Northern nuclear-free and possibly neutral zone been distasteful to the Soviet Union, the Finnish president would not have been able to return to the idea so frequently and over so many years.

Accordingly, neutrality as practised by Finland is a concept modified by circumstances and by neighbours. The strict observance of the letter in the earlier Finnish refusal to recognize either the East or West German Republics added nothing to the spirit. If it wished to survive as a democratic country, Finland had no choice but to bend its neutrality to suit the Soviet Union. The world can only admire and applaud the skill with which in this, as in other ways, it has made a virtue of necessity. Compromise can no longer be regarded as betrayal. Nevertheless, Finland had no obligation to seek to influence the rest of Scandinavia, and it may well be asked whether such an attitude is theoretically consistent with the practice of neutrality. Yet so far, the fruits of Finland's total attitude have been to the world's advantage. It has made possible a general relaxation of tension throughout the North, to which the Soviets, by abandoning Porkkala, and Norway and Denmark, by refusing American bases, have also made their contribution. No neutrality need be criticized for its imperfections if it yields such positive results.

Swedish neutrality comes in yet another version, different from both the Finnish and the Swiss. It demands participation in world affairs without commitment to any political grouping, and the security of adequate defence without commitment to any military grouping. It assumes non-alignment in peace-time and neutrality in war. Military security has been bought, as far as any country can buy it, by building up a highly efficient armaments industry, a well-developed defence force and the most extensive system of civilian protection enjoyed by any country in Western Europe. Thus the practical aspect has been handled with relative ease. By contrast, the policy of non-alignment requires a continuing series of balancing acts. These have included avoidance of any action likely to create tension between Finland and the Soviet Union; support for the United Nations in the Korean War through provision of a field hospital, but no combat units; membership of the Council of Europe conditional on the non-integration of the European Defence Community; and an entire range of qualifications in anticipation of a possible entry into EEC. Internal political attitudes have added a further dimension and tended to bias Sweden socially and economically. The Common Market, for instance, was at one time viewed and condemned as a prosperous bloc discriminating against the less fortunate. Finally, there is the growing problem of balancing official policy and public opinion. The present generation, more questioning and outspoken than its elders, is without inclination for total neutrality. Its influence has been felt in recent anti-American gestures. Its opposition to the Vietnam war has been shared all over the world, but the view has been expressed that official policy need not have gone to the non-neutral point of displaying greater sympathy with Hanoi than with Saigon. (In Europe, Sweden has diplomatic representation in West Germany, but does not recognize the People's Republic.) The Swedes rightly claim that they cannot satisfy everyone. Moreover, if they are allowed to condemn, for instance, the Soviet action in Czechoslovakia, they must also be free to criticize the United States. In the second half of the twentieth century, the posture of neutrality, even non-alignment, grows increasingly uncomfortable. Yet it has left the small Scandinavian countries with a luxury they have all enjoyed from time to time – the freedom to regard all great powers as the world's natural villains.

Denmark, Iceland and Norway, by comparison with Sweden and Finland, can follow a more straightforward path in international relations. Having opted to join NATO, their decisions must be largely made within its framework, and without the constant re-appraisal necessary to Finnish and Swedish decision-making. Although they have not always approved of the neutral attitudes of Sweden and the neutral approaches of Finland, NATO's Nordic states would be the first to admit that the policies of their eastern neighbours have considerably eased the inter-relationships of Scandinavia and the USSR.

Yet conflicting with the lingering inclination towards a modified neutrality is the will to co-operate, native to the Scandinavians nationally and now internationally. The Second World War and its aftermath lifted them out of the fringe attitude in which all, except Denmark, had tended to regard 'the Continent' as a near-separate entity. The desire to give help and to co-operate brought them into a far closer relationship than formerly both with the rest of Europe and with the world. Sweden's immediate post-war reaction was one of considerable generosity. Both government and private people made extensive credits and gifts to the other Scandinavian countries, the USSR, Germany and half a dozen other European countries. On the other hand, Sweden, along with Denmark, Iceland and Norway benefited from the Marshall Plan of 1948. Only Finland deemed it more prudent to hold back, in view of its then still precarious relationship with the Soviet Union. The extent of Finland's post-war recovery is made all the more remarkable by the fact that it was largely unaided, and handicapped by the massive reparations demanded by Russia. The European Recovery Programme gave practical impetus to the ideas and ideals of European unity then so widely discussed, and was followed by the launching of the various instruments and institutions intended to foster that unity. Denmark, Norway and Sweden all participated from the outset in the Council of Europe and in OECD. Iceland later joined both organizations. In 1961 Finland became an observer in a number of OECD activities, and in 1969 joined as a full member. It is not a member of the Council of Europe, but takes part in several of its cultural and non-political activities. Scandinavia also participated in a more individual way in the United Nations Economic Commission for Europe; the Swedish economist Gunnar Myrdal was its Executive Secretary for ten years, and was succeeded by Sakari Tuomioja of Finland.

It is in the United Nations that the Scandinavians have found their greatest opportunities of playing a constructive and often notable role in world affairs. Denmark and Norway were original charter members; Iceland and Sweden were admitted in 1946, and Finland in 1955. They have also found in it a means of furthering Nordic solidarity, without – for lack of size – appearing to form a power bloc. Their solidarity in the UN is a counterweight to their divergent individual foreign policies and external economic relationships. When the General Assembly is in session, the representatives of the Scandinavian countries meet regularly, often daily, to formulate a common policy. In difficult cases they do not feel obliged to strike attitudes or make propaganda for themselves; they merely abstain, singly or collectively, from registering their vote.

Even more important is the reputation which the Northern countries have gained in the world. All are exempted from suspicion of colonialism or neo-colonialism. All have impressed the developing countries with the help that they give. The West Europeans know them as strongholds of democracy. The USSR accepts them as neutral and semi-neutral. Thus it is not surprising that Scandinavia has twice provided the United Nations with a Secretary-General – the Norwegian Trygve Lie and the Swede Dag Hammarskjöld. It has also given three important mediators – Folke Bernadotte (Swedish), assassinated in Jerusalem by Jewish extremists in 1948; Sakari Tuomioja (Finnish), who died in 1964 while representing the UN in Cyprus; and Gunnar Jarring (Swedish), called to the superhuman task of mediating between Arab and Jew. Still another Swede, Per Jacobsen, was the first director of the International Monetary Fund – the branch of the UN which may be said to have done more to relieve world poverty than any other post-war institution. What is remarkable is that three small and allegedly 'little-known' countries should have been able to produce men of the considerable calibre needed to fill these demanding international offices. Neutrality is far from being enough to justify their appointments. The explanation lies partly in the rigorous educational standards demanded by the Scandinavians, in the ingrained social democracy that reduces prejudices and fears between man and man, and in the marked international orientation of Scandinavians as individuals, whatever their walk of life. As far back as 1920 Nansen had pointed the way in the League of Nations, where he was responsible for the passports for stateless people which bear his name.

At the same time as they have contributed leadership, the Scandinavians have participated actively in the UN peace-keeping forces. They maintain standby armed units ready to serve the UN immediately in any part of the world. In Cyprus, the Middle East, the Congo, Kashmir and Laos they have heightened their reputations, and neutrality has enabled the Swedes and the Finns, in particular, to act as observers and supervisors. But far more in accord with the natural bents and sympathies of the Scandinavians has been the technical assistance given by them to the developing countries. Their activities range from the small-scale, such as providing instruction and equipment for Indian fishermen, to large-scale joint programmes, such as the aid to Tanzania, and the common Nordic projects for East Africa. It is the more important that it is the Scandinavians who are helping to build up confidence in such areas. Africans, Asians and Latin Americans, coming to the Nordic countries as part of the programme of technical aid, can experience for themselves the attitudes of a group of countries striving to escape from what Stanley Anderson has called 'the closed circuit of national boundaries'.

The image that Scandinavia projects to most people is that of a community based on firm Lutheran foundations. This impression is strengthened by personal encounter with the Nordic countries. In their societies modernity is accompanied by reliability, social tolerance is balanced by social concern and energy is disciplined by education. Together with these qualities goes an element of self-righteousness which has caused commentators to observe Norway's tendency to regard itself as 'the keeper of the European conscience', and to detect in Swedish political life 'a yearning for the pulpit'. Puritan discipline accounts to some extent for the general suppression of emotion – save, perhaps, among the Finns. And when a sense of 'the tears of things' is lacking, so, often is outward joy or inward delight.

It would be unnatural if there were not reactions against the solid virtues derived from a puritan background. The mechanism of compensation partly explains the permissiveness, the pornography and the passions that occasionally break loose. The concept of the North as a 'clean, well-lighted place' has not gone unchallenged. Of course there are shortcomings; but they must be seen in a global perspective. In a world where the bare essentials of civilization are threatened, the Scandinavian countries draw their strength from a firm belief in their own ability to remain civilized and to contribute to the needs of others. There is abundant testimony to justify their belief.

Bibliography

Abraham, Gerald, *Grieg: A Symposium*, London, 1948.

Afzelius, N., *Books in English on Sweden*, Stockholm, 1951.

Allwood, M. S., *Twentieth-century Scandinavian Poetry*, Stockholm, 1951.

American-Scandinavian Review, New York, 1913–

Andersen, Hans Christian, *The Fairy Tale of My Life*, London, 1955.

Anderson, Stanley V., *The Nordic Council: A Study of Scandinavian Regionalism*, Stockholm, 1967.

Andersson, Ingvar, *A History of Sweden*, London, 1956.

Andrén, Nils, *Modern Swedish Government*, Stockholm, 1961; *Power Balance and Non-Alignment, A Perspective on Swedish Foreign Policy*, Stockholm, 1967.

Atlas of Denmark, Copenhagen, I, 1949; II, 1961.

Atlas of Finland, Helsinki, 1961.

Atlas of Sweden, Stockholm, 1953– .

Auden, W. H. and MacNeice, Louis, *Letters from Iceland*, London, 1938.

Bárdason, Hjalmar R., *Ice and Fire*, Reykjavik, 1971.

Berg, Jonas and Lagercrantz, Bo, *Scots in Sweden*, London, 1962.

Blegen, T. C., *The Norwegian Migration to America, 1825–60*, Northfield, Minn., 1931.

Blunt, Wilfrid, *The Compleat Naturalist: a life of Linnaeus*, London, 1971.

Boeson, Gudmund, *Danish Museums*, Copenhagen, 1966.

Branston, Brian, *Gods of the North*, London, 1968.

Bring, S., *Itineraria Svecana*, Uppsala, 1954.

Britten Austin, Paul, *Famous Swedes*, Stockholm, 1962; *On Being Swedish*, London, 1968.

Brøndsted, Johannes, *The Vikings*, London, 1960.

Campbell, Å., *Atlas of Swedish Folk Culture*, Uddevalla, 1957.

Capek, Karel, *Travels in the North*, London, 1939.

Castberg, Frede, *The Norwegian Way of Life*, London, 1952.

Childs, Marquis W., *Sweden: The Middle Way*, Yale, 1936.

Collinder, Björn, *The Lapps*, Princeton, 1949.

Connery, Donald S., *The Scandinavians*, London, 1966.

Drake, Michael, *Population and Society in Norway, 1735-1865*, Cambridge, 1969.

Ellison, J. Audrey, *The Great Scandinavian Cookbook*, London, 1966.

Fleisher, Frederic, *The New Sweden*, New York, 1967.

Foote, Peter, and Wilson, David M., *The Viking Achievement*, London, 1970.

Gad, Finn, *The History of Greenland*, London, 1969.

Glob, P. V., *The Bog People*, London, 1969.

Griffiths, John C., *Modern Iceland*, London, 1971.

Gustafson, Alrik, *A History of Swedish Literature*, Minneapolis, 1961.

Hagberg, Knut, *Carl Linnaeus*, London, 1952.

Hall, Wendy, *The Finns and their Country*, London, 1967.

Hallmundsson, Hallberg, *An Anthology of Scandinavian Literature*, New York, 1965.

Handbook of Denmark, Copenhagen, Danish Foreign Office, 1971.

Hatton, R. M., *Charles XII of Sweden*, London, 1967.

Heckscher, Eli, *An Economic History of Sweden*, Cambridge, Mass., 1954.

Heilborn, Adèle (ed.), *Travel, Study and Research in Sweden*, Stockholm, 1965.

Hoglund, W. A., *Finnish Immigrants in America, 1880–1920*, Madison, 1960.

Horton, John, *Scandinavian Music: A Short History*, London, 1963.

Hård af Segerstad, Ulf, *Scandinavian Design*, Helsinki, 1961.

Hövde, B. J., *The Scandinavian Countries, 1720–1865, The Rise of the Middle Classes*, New York, 1948.

Hunter, L. S., *Scandinavian Churches*, London, 1956.

Iceland 1966, Reykjavik, 1967.

Jakobson, Max, *The Diplomacy of the Winter War, 1939–40*, Cambridge, Mass., 1961; *Finnish Neutrality*, London, 1968.

Jenkins, David, *Sweden and the Price of Progress*, New York, 1968.

Johnson, Harold E., *Sibelius*, London, 1959.

Jones, Glyn W., *Denmark*, London, 1971.

Jones, Gwyn, *The Norse Atlantic Saga*, Oxford, 1964; *A History of the Vikings*, London 1968.

Jutikkala, E., *A History of Finland*, London, 1962.

Jörberg, Lennart, *Growth and Fluctuations of Swedish Industry, 1869–1912*, Lund, 1961; *The Industrial Revolution in Scandinavia 1850–1914*, London, 1970.

Kalevala, F. P. Magoun Jr. (Tr.), Cambridge, Mass., 1963.

Larsen, Karen, *A History of Norway*, New York, 1948.

Lauwerys, J. A. (ed.), *Scandinavian Democracy*, Copenhagen, 1958.

Lindgren, Raymond E., *Norwegian-Swedish Union, Disunion and Scandinavian Integration*, Princeton, 1959.

Lindroth, S. (ed.), *Swedish Men of Science*, Stockholm, 1952.

Lund, R. (ed.), *Scandinavian Adult Education*, Copenhagen, 1952.

Lyng, Jens, *The Scandinavians in Australia, New Zealand and the Western Pacific*, London, 1939.

Malmström, Vincent, *Norden, Crossroads of Destiny*, Princeton, 1965.

Mannerheim, C. G., *The Memoirs of Marshal Mannerheim*, London, 1953.

de Maré, Eric, *Scandinavia*, London, 1952.

Martin, A. J. and Wulfsberg, F., *Across the North Sea*, Oslo, 1955.

McFarlane, James, *Henrik Ibsen: A Critical Anthology*, London 1970.

Mead, W. R., *Finland*, London, 1968; *An Economic Geography of the Scandinavian States and Finland*, London, 1964; and Smeds, Helmer, *Winter in Finland*, London, 1968.

Meyer, Michael, *Henrik Ibsen*, 3 vols., London, 1967–71.

Miller, Kenneth, E., *Government and Politics in Denmark*, Boston, Mass., 1968.

Millward, Roy, *Scandinavian Lands*, London, 1964.

Mitchell, P. M., *History of Danish Literature*, Copenhagen, 1957.

Moberg, Vilhelm, *The Emigrants*, London, 1956; *Unto a Good Land*, London, 1957.

Modern Arts in Finland, a series in continuation published by Weidenfeld and Nicolson, London.

Mortensen, B. M. E. and Downs, B. W., *Strindberg: An Introduction to his Life and Work*, Cambridge, 1949.

Nelson, Helge, *The Swedes and Swedish Settlements in North America*, Lund, 1943.

Nickels, S. and Kallas, H. (ed.), *Finland, Creation and Construction*, London, 1968.

Nordic Co-operation, Nordic Council, Stockholm, 1965.

Nordisk utredningsserie, Expanded Nordic Economic Co-operation, Stockholm, 1969; *Nordic Economic and Cultural Co-operation*, Stockholm, 1970.

Nott, Kathleen, *A Clean, Well-lighted Place; A Private View of Sweden*, London, 1961.

Odhe, T., *Iceland, the Cooperative Island*, Chicago, 1960.

Paulsson, Thomas, *Scandinavian Architecture*, London, 1958.

Paulston, Rolland G., *Educational Change in Sweden*, New York, 1968.

Platt, R., *Finland and its Geography*, New York, 1955.

Richards, Denby, *The Music of Finland*, London, 1970.

Richards, J. M., *A Guide to Finnish Architecture*, London, 1966.

Roberts, M., *Gustavus Adolphus: A History of Sweden 1611–1632* (2 vols.), London, 1953–8; *Essays in Swedish History*, London, 1967; *The Early Vasas: A History of Sweden 1523–1611*, Cambridge, 1968.

Rosenthal, Albert H., *The Social Programs of Sweden*, Minneapolis, 1967.

Ruong, Israel, *The Lapps*, London, 1971.

Samuelson, K., *From Great Power to Welfare State*, London, 1968.

Sansom, William, *The Icicle and the Sun*, London, 1958.

Scandinavian Economic History Review, Stockholm, 1953–

Scott, Franklin D., *The United States and Scandinavia,* Cambridge, Mass., 1950.

Shirer, William L., *The Challenge of Scandinavia*, London, 1956.

Simpson, Colin, *The Viking Circle*, London, 1967.

Simpson, R., *Carl Nielsen*, London, 1952.

Skrubbeltrang, F. S., *Agricultural Reform and Rural Development in Denmark*, Rome, 1953.

Söderberg, Rolf, *Modern Swedish Art*, Stockholm, 1963.

Sømme, A. (ed.), *A Geography of Norden*, London, 1960.

Sturluson, Snorri, *Heimskringla: Sagas of the Norse Kings*, London, 1936.

Swedish Books, a series in continuation on various aspects of Swedish life, published by the Swedish Institute.

Tanner, Väinö, *The Winter War*, Oxford, 1957.

Tawaststjerna, Erik, *Jean Sibelius*, London, 1971.

Thorarinsson, S., *The Thousand Years Struggle Against Ice and Fire*, Reykjavik, 1956.

Turville-Petre, G., *The Heroic Age of Scandinavia*, London, 1951.

Undset, Sigrid, *Kristin Lavransdatter*, London, 1930.

Upton, A. F., *Finland in Crisis, 1940–41*, London, 1964.

Verney, Douglas, *Public Enterprise in Sweden*, Liverpool, 1959.

Vorren, Ö. (ed.), *Norway North of 65°*, London 1961.

Warner, Oliver, *A Journey to the Northern Capitals*, London, 1968.

Wendt, Frantz, *The Nordic Council and Co-operation in Scandinavia*, Copenhagen, 1959.

West, John F., *Faroe, The Emergence of a Nation*, London, 1971.

Wilhelm, Prince of Sweden, *This Land of Sweden*, Stockholm, 1958.

Williamson, Kenneth, *The Atlantic Islands*, London, 1970.

Wilson, D. M. and Klindt-Jensen, O., *Viking Art*, London, 1966.

Wizelius, Ingemar (ed.), *Sweden in the Sixties*, Stockholm, 1967.

Wuorinen, John H., *A History of Finland*, New York, 1965.

Yearbook of Nordic Statistics, Annually.

Zahle, Erik, *Scandinavian Domestic Design*, London, 1963.

Who's Who

AALTO, Alvar (b. 1898). Leading Finnish architect and town-planner, member of the Academy of Finland. His buildings in the USA, Germany, Italy and other European countries, as well as Finland, have influenced modern architecture all over the world. He has also designed furniture and lighting equipment.

AMUNDSEN, Roald (1872–1928). Norwegian Arctic and Antarctic explorer. He discovered the South Pole in 1911 only a few days before it was reached by Captain Scott's expedition. He made various attempts to reach the North Pole by sea and by air, and passed over it in an airship in 1926. He lost his life in 1928, in an air attempt to rescue survivors from an Italian airship which had crashed in Arctic seas. His own plane disappeared and was never found.

ANDERSEN, Hans Christian (1805–1875). Danish author of the famous fairy tales which have tended to overshadow his vast output of novels, poems and plays. He was born to a poor family in Odense (Fyn), where there is now an H. C. Andersen Museum. His wide journeyings abroad are recorded in a number of travel books; while in England he spent several weeks in Charles Dickens's home.

BJÖRNSON, Björnstjerne (1832–1910). Norwegian poet, novelist and dramatist; awarded Nobel prize for literature, 1903. His early work was set against a peasant background, but he later turned to realism, exploring personal and social problems. He was active politically and socially, a champion of Norwegian independence, and writer of the words of the Norwegian national anthem.

BOHR, Niels (1885–1962). Danish physicist, Nobel prizewinner (1922), and participator in the development of the atomic bomb. He spent several years in Britain with J. J. Thomson and Lord Rutherford studying the structure of the atom. In 1920 he became director of the Institute of Theoretical Physics in Copenhagen, and held this post until his death in 1962.

There he made a major contribution to atomic research. He escaped from Denmark to the USA during the Second World War. Although involved in the development of the atomic bomb, he worked incessantly from 1944 onwards for the promotion of peace and the control of nuclear weapons.

BRAHE, Tycho (1546–1601). Danish astronomer, discoverer of a 'new star' (nova) in the constellation Cassiopeia, still known as 'Tycho's star'. Working with Kepler, who edited his principal work, he made a considerable contribution to scientific developments.

BRANTING, Karl Hjalmar (1860–1925). Swedish statesman, one of the founders of the Social Democratic party, and its first and only representative in the Swedish parliament from 1896 to 1902. He became Prime Minister in the first Social Democratic government in 1920, and in two subsequent governments. As a neutral internationalist, he was a delegate to the Paris peace conference of 1919, and Swedish representative at the League of Nations. He was awarded the Nobel peace prize in 1921.

GRIEG, Edvard (1843–1907). Norway's greatest composer, and representative of the nineteenth-century romantic school. He is known particularly for his A minor piano concerto and the incidental music for Ibsen's *Peer Gynt* and for Björnson's *Sigurd Jorsalfar*. He was deeply attached to Norwegian folk music, which he absorbed into his own musical personality, and which is reflected in his many arrangements and songs.

GRUNDTVIG, N. F. S. (1783–1872). Danish ecclesiast who left a lasting mark on adult education throughout Scandinavia. He is known both as the 'father of the folk high school', and as the founder of Grundtvigianism, an important revivalist trend in the Danish church. Grundtvig eventually became a bishop, after having taken an active part in the introduction of parliamentary government in Denmark. He also achieved some distinction as a student of old Norse literature, as a poet, and as a writer of hymns.

HAMMARSKJÖLD, Dag (1905–1961). Swedish Secretary-General of the United Nations (1953–1961), and son of a former Prime Minister of Sweden. Before joining the UN he held important posts in the Swedish home and foreign service. To the office of Secretary-General of the UN he gave an individual and positive turn, imposing his own sense of leadership on the organization. He was killed when his plane crashed when visiting the warring Congo in 1961. Personally, he was detached and mystical, as revealed in his posthumously published diary, *Markings*.

HOLBERG, Ludvig (1684–1754). Norwegian-born writer and scholar who settled in Denmark, and became known as the founder of Danish literature. At a time when French and German were the languages of literature and the drama in Denmark, he wrote a series of comedies in Danish for the first Danish Theatre in Copenhagen. He wrote histories and satires, poems and essays. Of him it has been said: 'Holberg found Denmark provided with no books, and he wrote a library for it.'

IBSEN, Henrik (1828–1906). Norwegian who is considered today as one of the great dramatists of all time. To his technical mastery and gift of poetry, he added a social and psychological insight which made him the pioneer of the modern realistic drama. Like so many Scandinavian writers and artists, he felt the need for wider European contacts, and spent much of his life in Germany and Italy. Likewise, much of his work reflects a reaction against narrow Norwegian society. 'Social' plays such as *Pillars of Society, A Doll's House*, and *Ghosts* touched off, inside and outside Norway, violent pro and anti reactions; together with his other works, they changed the course of European drama, and inspired his British disciple, George Bernard Shaw.

JACOBSEN, Per (1894–1963). Swedish economist and managing director of the International Monetary Fund, 1956–63. After lecturing in economics at the Stockholm Schools of Forestry and Engineering, he joined the economic and financial section of the League of Nations in 1920. Subsequently he served for 25 years in the Bank of International Settlements.

JARRING, Gunnar (b. 1907). Swedish diplomat and UN mediator between the Jews and Arabs since the 1967 war. He joined the Swedish Ministry for Foreign Affairs in 1940, and has been head of its political department, as well as Swedish ambassador to the United Nations, to the USA, and to the Soviet Union.

KEKKONEN, Urho Kaleva (b. 1900). President of the Republic of Finland since 1956. He had previously been Prime Minister five times, as leader of the Centre (formerly Agrarian) party, a member of several governments and a director of the Bank of Finland. Outside politics, he is known as a sportsman and athlete of some distinction.

KIERKEGAARD, Søren (1813–1855). Danish theologian and philosopher whose system anticipates the work of modern existentialists. He took up a position of hostility to both the established church in Denmark and the Hegelian rationalization of Christianity. His output, published under his own name and pseudonyms, was extremely large; his best-known work is *Either/Or*, which deals with the choice between Christ and the world.

KIVI, Aleksis (1834–1872). Finnish author and playwright; one of the earliest Finns to use the Finnish rather than the Swedish language as a literary vehicle. His most famous novel, *Seven Brothers*, has become a classic story of the social conflict between the brothers and the village community.

LAGERLÖF, Selma (1858–1940). Swedish novelist and the first woman to be awarded the Nobel prize. She was primarily a fine storyteller who made her reputation with romantic historical novels. The first of these was *Gösta Berlings Saga*; another notable long novel is *Jerusalem*.

LAXNESS, Halldor (b. 1902). Iceland's leading writer, awarded the Nobel prize for literature in 1955. After living several years in France and USA he settled in his own country to write both historical and contemporary novels based on Icelandic life. He is said to have restored the Icelandic language as an instrument for storytelling.

LIE, Trygve (b. 1896). Norwegian statesman and first Secretary-General of the United Nations, 1946–52. He had previously been a leading Labour party lawyer in Norway, and from 1940, foreign minister of the Norwegian government-in-exile. As UN Secretary-General he is remembered principally for his firm support of UN military action in Korea.

LINNAEUS, Carolus (Carl von Linné) (1707–1778). Swedish botanist, 'King of Flowers', who defined the principles of classification of genera and species of plants. He also classified animals and minerals. He started his career as a physician, became professor of medicine at Uppsala University, and later, professor of botany. During his lifetime he published more than 180 works, including *Flora Lapponica, Flora Suecica, Fauna Suecica*, and, most important of all, *Species Plantarum*. His *Lapland Journey* (English translation, 1816) established a tradition of topographical writing.

MANNERHEIM, Gustaf (1867–1951). Marshal of Finland, whose leadership of the Finnish forces in the Winter War (1939–40) has made him an almost legendary figure. He began service in the Russian Imperial Army in 1897; was Regent of Finland, 1918–19; chairman of the Defence Council from 1931, and President of the Republic, 1944–46.

MUNCH, Edvard (1863–1944). Norwegian painter and a leading figure of the expressionism movement. During his early career he was preoccupied with symbolic and psychological themes, but eventually turned to more naturalistic landscapes, portraits and figure compositions. He was also responsible for murals in Oslo University assembly hall. A special gallery is devoted to his works in Oslo.

MYRDAL, Gunnar (b. 1898). Swedish economist, sociologist and cabinet minister, and executive secretary of the UN Economic Commission for Europe, 1947–57. He is noted for his sociological and anthropological study *An American Dilemma: the Negro Problem and Modern Democracy* (1944). His wife, Alva, has held positions in the UN and UNESCO, served as Swedish ambassador to India, headed the Swedish delegation to the Geneva disarmament conference and been a member of the Swedish cabinet.

NANSEN, Fridtjof (1861–1930). Norwegian explorer and scientist, awarded the Nobel peace prize in 1922. Crossed Greenland on skis 1888–89, commissioned Arctic exploration ship *Fram* and explored Arctic Ocean 1893–96. Published *Farthest North* (1897), *In Northern Mists* (1911). He later turned to political life, and became Norwegian minister to London, 1906–08. He led the Norwegian delegation to the first Assembly of the League of Nations in 1920, where he was responsible for the repatriation of prisoners-of-war, international famine relief, and the introduction of the 'Nansen passport' for displaced and stateless persons.

NIELSEN, Carl (1865–1931). Danish composer who achieved world-wide renown. He is known particularly for his six richly scored symphonies, but also composed three concertos, two operas and four string quartets, among numerous other works.

NOBEL, Alfred (1833–1896). Swedish inventor of dynamite and founder of the Nobel prizes. From the manufacture of dynamite and other explosives, and also from the exploitation of oilfields in Baku, he accumulated a large fortune. The bulk of this was left at his death to a trust to establish five prizes for work in the promotion of peace, physics, chemistry, physiology or medicine, and literature.

NORDENSKJÖLD, Otto (1869–1928). Swedish geographer and explorer, whose Antarctic expedition of 1901–03 yielded important scientific results. He also made expeditions to Greenland, Peru and Patagonia. He was appointed to the chair of geography at Gothenburg University in 1903, and became, in 1923, the first rector of the Gothenburg school of advanced commercial studies.

NURMI, Paavo (b. 1897). Finnish athlete, and international champion runner of the nineteen-twenties. At one time he held 24 world records, including the mile and the marathon.

PAASIKIVI, Juho Kusti (1870–1956). President of the Republic of Finland from 1946 to 1956. He had been Prime Minister in 1918, and Finnish minister to Stockholm 1936–40, and to Moscow 1940–41. He was chiefly responsible for the negotiations which withdrew Finland from the war with Russia in 1944, and the architect of the 'good-neighbour' policy towards the Soviet Union, first as Prime Minister from 1944 to 1946, and then as President of the Republic. He managed to remain unusually aloof from party politics.

RUNEBERG, Johan Ludvig (1804–1877). Finnish 'national' poet, best known for his cycle *Tales of Ensign Stål* (translated into English), dealing with the Russo-Finnish war of 1808–9. The Finnish national anthem *Our Land* is taken from the opening poem. *King Fjalar*, also translated into English, is a Viking epic inspired by the panScandinavian movement of the time.

SAARINEN, Eliel (1873–1950). The first Finnish architect to exert a major influence on building outside Finland. His work in Finland, in particular Helsinki railway station, belongs to the national romantic style; when he moved to the USA in 1922 he turned to functionalism, and had a marked influence on the development of the skyscraper. His son Eero, an American citizen, was the architect of the American Embassy in London.

SIBELIUS, Jean (1865–1957). Finland's greatest composer, at one time called its 'uncrowned king'. Through his earlier works – notably *Finlandia* – he was associated with the national romantic movement; but the originality of his seven symphonies and his violin concerto established his permanent world stature. Although his output over many years was considerable, he published no further compositions after the tone poem *Tapiola* in 1925, and the incidental music to Shakespeare's *The Tempest* in 1926.

STEFANSSON, Vilhjalmur (1879–1962). Arctic explorer, born in Canada of Icelandic parents. He became an authority on the Canadian Arctic, where he discovered three islands; and on the Eskimos, among whom he lived for a year. He became consultant on Arctic operations to Pan American Airways in 1932, and during the Second World War advised the US government on defence conditions in Alaska.

STRINDBERG, August (1849–1912). The greatest Swedish playwright, also novelist, short-story writer and poet. A social, political and literary rebel, he led a disturbed emotional life, and went through a period of mental instability. Through his plays he influenced the development of the drama throughout Europe; and through his prose style he revivified Swedish writing. His plays have been translated into several languages; among those best known in the English-speaking world are *The Father, Lady Julie, A Dream Play* and *The Ghost Sonata*.

SWEDENBORG, Emanuel (1688–1772). Swedish scientist, philosopher and theologian. For 30 years he was assessor to the Royal College of Mines, and played an important part in the development of the Swedish metal-mining industry. Although his scientific works, particularly those dealing with physics, were far ahead of his time, he is principally known as a theologian. He rejected belief in the Trinity, asserting the absolute unity of God, and arguing in a rational manner which contrasts with his more mystical personal approach to religion. His best-known work is *Heaven and Hell*, published in London in 1758.

UNDSET, Sigrid (1882–1949). Norwegian writer and Nobel prizewinner who achieved fame through her three-volume medieval novel *Kristin Lavransdatter* (1920–22). A period of office work in early life gave her an insight, revealed in several novels, into the difficulties of the lower-class working girl. Her interest in history led to *Kristin Lavransdatter* and *Olav Audunssön*, also set in medieval Norway. Finally her conversion to Roman Catholicism influenced her later novels, of which most have a contemporary background.

VIGELAND, Adolf Gustav (1869–1943). Norway's leading sculptor, who spent much of his life working on the vast collection contained in the several acres of Frogner Park, Oslo. Here an enormous number of single figures and groups are intended to portray the history of mankind, from barbarism to civilization.

Acknowledgments

Finnish Embassy, 6, 7, 12, 17, 22, 23, 29, 31; Georg Jensen, 31; Icelandic Government Information Service, 9; Icelandic Tourist Information Bureau, 3, 10, 26, 27; National Museum of Antiquities, Copenhagen, I; Nordisk Pressefoto, 4, 8; Normanns Kunstforlag, 18; Royal Danish Embassy, 2; Royal Danish Ministry for Foreign Affairs 24, 25; Royal Norwegian Embassy, 5, 13, 15, 19, 31; The Swedish Institute, 11, 16, 21, 30, 31; Tiofoto, 20; Universitetets Oldsaksamling, Oslo, 28

Index